All Things are Nothing to Me

The Unique Philosophy of Max Stirner

All Things are Nothing to Me

The Unique Philosophy of Max Stirner

Jacob Blumenfeld

Winchester, UK
Washington, USA

First published by Zero Books, 2018
Zero Books is an imprint of John Hunt Publishing Ltd., No. 3 East St., Alresford,
Hampshire SO24 9EE, UK
office1@jhpbooks.net
www.johnhuntpublishing.com
www.zero-books.net

For distributor details and how to order please visit the 'Ordering' section on our website.

Text copyright: Jacob Blumenfeld 2017

ISBN: 978 1 78099 663 9
978 1 78535 895 1 (ebook)
Library of Congress Control Number: 2017958217

A CIP catalogue record for this book is available from the British Library.

Design: Stuart Davies

Printed and bound by CPI Group (UK) Ltd, Croydon, CR0 4YY, UK

We operate a distinctive and ethical publishing philosophy in
all areas of our business, from our global network of authors to
production and worldwide distribution.

Contents

Introduction

Max Stirner's *Der Einzige und sein Eigentum* (1844)[1] is the first ruthless critique of modern society. Misunderstood, dismissed, and defamed, it is now time to unearth this savage book once more. My aim is to reconstruct the unique philosophy of Max Stirner (1806–1856), a figure that strongly influenced—for better or worse—Karl Marx, Friedrich Nietzsche, Emma Goldman as well as numerous anarchists, feminists, surrealists, illegalists, existentialists, fascists, libertarians, dadaists, situationists, insurrectionists and nihilists of the last two centuries.

Translated into English incorrectly as *The Ego and Its Own*,[2] Stirner's work is considered by some to be the worst book ever written. It combines the worst elements of philosophy, politics, history, psychology, and morality, and ties it all together with simple tautologies, fancy rhetoric, and militant declarations. That is the glory of Max Stirner's unique footprint in the history of philosophy.

In exhuming this philosophical corpse, however, I have discovered Stirner's spirit already living among us. I have thus conducted a forensic investigation into how his thought has stayed un-dead through time. The results of this investigation are contained herein.

Stirner's anti-moral, anti-political, and anti-social philosophy is especially in vogue today, in a hyperpolarized, post-crisis world where god, government and the good have all died, replaced by technology, markets and private interest. Stirner's "egoistic" philosophy at first seems compatible with this neoliberal nightmare, and surely enough, his once-sketched face has been revived as a meme, popping up in the stranger corners of the Internet. As one of the first trolls to ridicule everything sacred in modern life, to praise the transgression of all social norms, values and customs, Stirner may even be seen as a

1

harbinger of today's edgy alt-right.[3] But that is just one of many Stirners, a rather superficial one at best. What I hope to show is another Stirner—contemporary, critical, useful.

As a piercing critic of social alienation and political ideology, perhaps a better analogy for Stirner today would be the *Invisible Committee*, that band of heretical communists and anarchists who rage against the insufferable liberalism, identitarianism, and pseudoactivism of today's left.[4] Like them, Stirner defends insurrection, advocates crime, and incites individuals to find each other in free unions or communes that can expand one's power against the state.

Stirner's philosophy is a big fuck you to every progressive and liberal viewpoint. It is not expressed in the name of some superior tradition, race, gender, or nationality. Fuck them all, Stirner says, and fuck you too. I don't care about your values, your issues, your cause—I care about *me*. Only after we learn how to care for ourselves can we begin to care for each other as singular equals, and not as generic representatives of groups, classes, identities, and states. That is Stirner's provocation.

In Part I, I supply preliminary material necessary for approaching Stirner before delving straight into his writing. In this section, I include a review of past attempts to account for why his spirit has remained un-dead. My initial conclusion is that all these accounts are stuck in a historicist paradigm. At first, they try to bury Stirner within *his* own time. If that fails, then they attempt to bury him within *their* own time. Either way, he is submerged by time—but his spirit escapes again. I also provide some of my own findings on alternative ways for tracking Stirner, ones that consider his practical, performative, and ethical dimension. Finally, I begin chasing Stirner's ghost, but end up barely catching a thing. Yet I do discover something interesting, namely, that one does not need the concept of the "ego" to understand Stirner at all. In fact, this might have been the biggest stumbling block towards making sense of his philosophy.

In Part II, I begin reading Stirner's text properly, focusing on the first part of *Der Einzige*, called "Der Mensch," or *Man*. I lay out the basic rhetorical devices used by Stirner, focusing especially on how "spooks" are made. This part deals mostly with Stirner's logic of alienation and reification. Next, I explain how these devices function in the realms of psychology, philosophy and history. Where others see bad dialectics, I see good allegories, parodies, and satire. This section ends with an analysis of Stirner's critique of liberalism, socialism, and humanism.

In Part III, I present a comprehensive interpretation of Stirner's erratic thinking. Following my own rules, I reconstruct Stirner's argument piece by piece, sometimes independently of his own claims. I weave together the main theses of Stirner's positive argument concerning his so-called "egoism" in a winding route, based mostly within Part II of *Der Einzige*, called "Ich" or *I*. This section dives right into the stranger parts of Stirner, including his theories of individuality, property, power, owners, ownness, consumption, dissolution, self-annihilation, nothingness, the unique, the state, the union, secession and insurrection. Throughout the analysis, I sharpen the argument with philosophical digressions from other thinkers who come within eyesight of Stirner's ghost as well. This includes Stoics, Spinoza, Nietzsche, Heidegger, Foucault, Derrida, Levinas, Landauer, and Debord. Finally, I place Stirner in dialogue with his fiercest critic, Marx, and show the points of contact between them concerning individualism and communism. This allows us to read Stirner anew once more, from the beginning.

Notes

1. "Max Stirner" is the pseudonym of Johann Kaspar Schmidt. *Der Einzige und sein Eigentum* was translated into English in 1907 as *The Ego and Its Own* by Steven T. Byington, under the tutelage of Benjamin R. Tucker. The translation used here

is the 1995 version reedited by David Leopold, published by Cambridge University Press. Cited as EO from now. I frequently change the translation to be more accurate, for instance rendering "*Ich*" as I instead of Ego.

2. A wonderful new translation by Wolfi Landstreicher, entitled *The Unique and Its Property* (2018), has remedied this error, and many others. Unfortunately, it appeared after the main portion of this text was written, and so it will not be referenced.

3. On the "transgressive" nature of the alt-right, see Nagle, *Kill All Normies* (2017).

4. See, for instance, *The Coming Insurrection* (2009).

Part I: Stirner's Revenge

Reading Max Stirner

Stirner is a product of his time, they say. So let us trace his roots and legacy.

Who is Max Stirner? First reading: a young Hegelian, the ultimate culmination of Hegel's philosophy, his disciple and destroyer.[1] How is he both disciple and destroyer? The philosophy of Hegel proceeds dialectically, through the power of negation. In an incredibly intricate manner, the cunning of reason, whether in objective history as spirit or subjective consciousness as concept, elegantly progresses through stages, experiences, and thoughts until it hits a limit, gap or contradiction. This contradiction, when recognized, can negate or cancel that which initially grounded it. Another negation, one which confronts the confrontation of the original ground, propels the initial negation toward an intrinsic resolution. This determinate negation is positive, carrying within it the insight, history, and meaning of that which it negated into its new form. This dialectical logic of movement, propelled by contradiction, is repeatedly expressed in different guises throughout Hegel's analyses. From the negation of sense-certainty by consciousness to the negation of the master by the slave to the negation of religion by absolute knowledge, the negative works its way, like a vector, through all being.

However, with any consistent system there emerges a skeptical worry about a fundamental paradox: does the system belong to itself? In essence, we can ask Hegel the same question: does the system submit to its own logic? If it does, then should it not also hit a limit, a contradiction which lays bare its negative potential for overcoming? If so, then the process of dialectical logic *itself* would cease to be valid, since the dialectic would be subsumed under its own treatment. Dialectical dialectics, in other words, critical critique would produce... nothing, absolutely nothing. For the negation would be absolute, as will the object of its negation. If we place Hegel's system within the limit of the person named "Hegel", then we can resolve this by stating that Hegel himself is the absolute limit, the absolute self-consciousness with absolute knowledge of the absolute idea in absolute time. But, if we abstract the system from the man, and allow it to have a life of its own, then the problem compounds. Not Hegel but Hegelianism as a system is then submitted to its own dialectical logic. If that is true, then who stars in the acting roles of its negation?

First negation: the left, young Hegelians. Already with Feuerbach, Hess, and Bauer, we hit the limit of Hegel's speculative project. The self-described "pure critique" or "critical critique" targets the theological aspects of Hegelianism as well as its political conservatism. The young Hegelians begin the descent into the metaphysics of materialism and politics of humanist socialism.

Second negation: Max Stirner. Not only philosophically but historically bringing to an end the "young Hegelian" consensus, Stirner is the perfect candidate for the title of *absolute negation* of *absolute negation*. Ending the short-lived reign of humanism, Stirner rejects all attempts at a synthesis with social, material, or human "essences."

New trajectory: Marx, who turns Hegel right side up, is the third term which opens up a new positive phase in the process, only made possible by the previous negations.

In this drama, Stirner occupies a mediating role as the catalyst who caused a paradigm shift in Hegel's wake. This shift allowed Marx to make a conceptual breakthrough towards "historical materialism". That is one story, but problems are easy to note. First off, why would this process remain *dialectical*? In principle, it should not, for this is supposed to be the story of the overcoming of dialectic. The transition from Hegel to Feuerbach,

Feuerbach to Stirner, and Stirner to Marx should then not be seen as dialectical, for then the dialectic was not truly relinquished. Any trace of determinate negation would signal life to that which must have died. Second, even if we accept this account, can one really claim that Marx initiated a completely new sequence of thought? Marx surely transformed the content of dialectic in his analysis of political economy, yet he nonetheless retained the form of the dialectical method itself. Dialectic then did not die, only changed focus.

Second try: who is Max Stirner? Nothing more than an expression of the *petty bourgeoisie*. A failed student, failed teacher, failed journalist, failed translator, failed husband, and a failed businessman—Stirner was even jailed in a debtors' prison, twice. His attempted milk delivery business, funded by his wife's inheritance, collapsed because he forgot to advertise it to potential customers.[2] Stirner's philosophy of egoism can thus be seen as an ideological reflection of his economic struggle to join the bourgeoisie. This is the classic communist reading of Stirner and—for that matter—of all the anarchists of the 19th (and 20th) century by Marx, Engels and their followers. Proudhon, Bakunin, Stirner: who are they but mouthpieces of the petty shopkeepers that want to retain their "individual" capital? The bold pronouncements about the "uniqueness" and "individuality" of the ego are nothing but cries of fear and shouts of reaction against the rising swell of communism. Incapable of thinking beyond the bourgeois category of the idealized individual, Stirner should therefore be excluded from revolutionary discussion and activity. And so, Marx produced a four-hundred-page ruthless criticism of Stirner in the notebooks that became *The German Ideology*, similar in that sense (but not nearly in scope) to what was done to Proudhon in *The Poverty of Philosophy*, to what Marx was planning with Bakunin's *Statism and Anarchy*, and to what Engels did to the anarchists in his *Socialism: Utopian and Scientific*.

Does this perspective hold any water? If class background determined the validity of one's ideas, then Marx and Engels themselves would have no credibility either. Or does this critique mean something different, namely that no matter the background of the person, the ideas themselves are *petty bourgeois*? This is surely possible with Stirner, since his ideas have been historically appropriated by self-described anarcho-capitalists, right-wing libertarians and fascists. However, his work has also been appropriated by left-wing socialists, bohemians, and feminists. This is the fate of all great works, and to condemn a text for opening the door to many uses precludes the potential for conflicting interpretations. Is not even Marx's *Capital* read today on Wall Street?

This *ad hominem* refrain, which reduces one's ideas to the ideological expressions of one's material conditions, has been repeated throughout history against the anarchists. It does not really amount to anything more than the fear of losing one's political hegemony to other radical positions. It was Engels who first boxed Stirner in with the anarchists in his *Ludwig Feuerbach and the Outcome of Classical German Philosophy*, by stating (questionably) that he was a major influence on Bakunin. This was meant to discredit Bakunin, of course, for who would want to share company with the lunatic Max Stirner?

A century and a half after *The German Ideology* was penned, Derrida attempted to unravel the tangled web of ghosts that haunted both Stirner and Marx.[3] Yet even there Derrida only reads Stirner with and against Marx in that great *phantomachia*. Perhaps, as he urges, it is time to "take seriously the originality, audacity, and precisely, the philosophico-political seriousness of Stirner who also should be read without Marx or against him."[4]

Try again, who is Max Stirner? Third reading: solipsist. In one of the two main books that would locate Stirner within the history of Western philosophy,[5] Eduard Von Hartmann's 1869 *Philosophy of the Unconscious* makes the claim that Stirner's egoism is nothing but a radicalized Fichtean philosophy, one which works through tautology (I am I! You are you!). Although tempting, this interpretation should be firmly rejected. According to Hartmann, this solipsistic philosophy inevitably leads to a morality based on the "libertinage of the sovereign caprice of the individual" [*Libertinage der souveranen Laune des Individuums*].[6] This view is shared by Martin Buber who, in *Between Man and Man*, contrasts Kierkegaard with Stirner. In the chapter, "Question to the Single One [*Einzige*]," Buber concludes that, although Stirner and Kierkegaard share many affinities (both are radical critics of Hegel who emphasize singular existence over abstract essence), Stirner's "egoism" gets us nowhere.[7]

Once more, who is Max Stirner? Fourth reading: nihilist. The only monograph in the English language to deal with Max Stirner up until 1976 was RWK Paterson's *The Nihilistic Egoist Max Stirner*. Reading Stirner as the first full philosophical expression of nihilism *in its own terms*, Paterson takes Stirner's position to be one of pure negation, impressive for its audacity but dangerous in its implications. Nihilism in this sense is *moral* nihilism.

Yet there is another reading of Stirner *qua* nihilist that is perhaps more productive here. In his *Nietzsche and Philosophy* (1969), Deleuze bestows high praise on Stirner for being the "dialectician who reveals nihilism as the truth of the dialectic."[8] By taking the dialectic to the extreme, Stirner pushed it until the essence of dialectic was revealed: a pure I which, in the end, is nothingness itself. How is this so? Although the speculative logic of the dialectic is contradiction and resolution, its practical motor is alienation and reappropriation.[9] In order to put the dialectic to a stop, an absolute appropriation is needed, one which allows for *nothing* to escape, for "relative appropriations are still absolute alienations."[10] By becoming *proprietor*, I the owner consume the dialectic into my own being, dissolving all ideas and objects into myself before they can escape again. This dissolution occurs in the I, *as* the I. Even I must relate to myself as pure nothing so that I do not escape into something alienable. As Deleuze puts it, "history in general and Hegelianism in particular found their outcome, but also their most complete dissolution, in a triumphant nihilism. Dialectic loves and controls history, but it has a history itself which it suffers from and which it does not control. The meaning of history and the dialectic together is not the realization of reason, freedom, or man as species, but nihilism, nothing but nihilism."[11] This then is the meaning of Stirner's "unique one." For Deleuze, this was a powerful move, but one which Nietzsche ultimately surpassed with his quest for affirmation outside of any discussion of "property." Stirner was all too *reactive*, not light enough for a truly gay spirit.

Who is Max Stirner? Fifth reading: not the last Hegelian but the first poststructuralist.[12] Reading Stirner's philosophy as an epistemological critique of *essences* instead of a metaphysical exposition of reality, some recent philosophers have situated Stirner's project within and beyond a poststructuralist framework. Assimilated into French philosophy, Stirner can now be read alongside Lacan, Derrida, Foucault, and Deleuze in their unified assault on the traditional Western metaphysical concepts of truth, history and subjectivity. Although this reading is interesting for its contemporary relevance, it levels the nuances of Stirner's argument, as well as the differences between all those other subsumed philosophers.

More? Sixth, existentialist.[13] Seventh, individualist anarchist.[14] Eighth, proto-right-wing libertarian.[15] Ninth, fascist.[16] Tenth, insane.[17] Eleventh, twelfth... *Man, our head is spooked! How many more can we fit in here?* Our "earthly apartments" are becoming "badly overcrowded."[18] Which spooks then should we evict? How about all of them? Fine, no more wheels in the head.

What dogma unites all these "Stirner studies"? Simply put, *historicism*. By historicism I mean the tendency to reduce one's work (or thought) to a *necessary* result of a socioeconomic, political, and philosophical aggregate which one can call "historical context" or "age." Stirner is a product of his *age*, his *times* — 1840s, Berlin, Germany — which were, of course, dominated by Hegelianism and its followers, the critique of theology, France's revolutionary legacy, burgeoning industrial capitalism, the dominance of liberalism and the opening breaths of socialism and so on.

Stirner himself exposed the fallacy of historicism. In relation to Feuerbach's doctrine of *sensualism*, he asked: what makes someone uniquely who they are? What makes a person *singular*, *this* one, and not another? Sensuousness can be a condition of my identity, but not a determinate factor of who I am. Ventriloquizing Hegel, he asks, "If I were not this one, for instance, Hegel, I should not look at the world as I do look at it, I should not pick out of it that philosophical system which just I, as Hegel, do."[19] Can we perhaps extend this to materialism, empiricism, and historicism? To Stirner, any theory which only considers the aggregate of conditions (e.g. senses, matter, facts) from which something emerges will never be able to fully show how that emergent something *became itself* in its singularity. An analysis of historical, empirical conditions will only tell us the clothing that such a singularity wears.

Stirner rejects philosophical determinism, including the claim that every action must have some identifiable cause which can be reconstructed in principle. But Stirner does not retreat into religion, declaring that something can come from nothing, *ex nihilo*, since that is how God works, for instance. But is there a third option? A rigorously atheistic rejection of determinism which does not lapse into mysticism or the absurd? It is here, on the edge of an abyss, where Stirner proclaims the idea of the *creative nothing* [*schöpferische Nichts*], "the nothing out of which I myself as creator create everything."[20] For Stirner, there is always an excess of being that outstrips the possibility for conceptual capture in a regime of representation. Excess is a misleading word, since Stirner's *Eigenheit* also refers to that which is *below*

11

or *underneath*, that which lacks the full presence of a mediating concept.

The idea of the *un-man* [*Unmensch*] animates this point. What is the un-man? "It is a man who does not correspond to the *concept* man, as the inhuman is something human which does not conform to the *concept* of the human."[21] Not someone other than myself as human, but that part of myself which is not explainable by my "humanness" or species qualifications. I am un-man when I exceed, fall short, disrupt, cancel, or displace myself from being interpreted through the grid of the concept *man, human being*. Stirner's un-man makes the point that *my humanness* is an amoral category, a manipulation of biological taxonomy for political justifications of power. The un-man is that *homo sacer* which founds and negates the liberal project of human rights. It is that *real* part of me which cannot be symbolized in any order, yet which structures the symbolic order as such. The un-man does not just ring the morning bell of the "death of man", but rather it signifies that supplement which binds itself to any essentializing logic. Go ahead and posit *man*, Stirner seems to say, but know that it is not I, for I am either too much or too little for any such category. I am, in a sense, *subtracted* from man, not because I desire something else, but because I have no desire to fulfill the imposed criteria of humanity.

In a defense of Stirner, most likely written by Stirner himself in 1847, "G. Edward" captures this rage against the category of the human:

Against this phrase of 'humanism', Stirner posits the phrase of 'egoism'. How? You summon me to be a 'human being'; more precisely, that I should be 'man'? Well! I was already a 'human being', 'bare homunculus' and 'man' in the cradle; that is what I am for sure; but I am more than that, I am what I have become through myself, my own development, by the appropriation of the outside world, of history, etc. I am unique.

But that is not what you really want. You do not want me to be a real man, you do not give a penny for my uniqueness. You want me to be 'man', as you have constructed him, as an ideal for all. You want to make the 'loutish principle of equality' the standard of my life. Principle around principle! Demand around demand! I posit the principle of egoism against you. I just want to be 'I', to despise nature, men and their laws, human society and their love, and cut loose from every general relation, even the one of language, with you. Against all the impressions of your 'ought', all designations of your categorical judgments, I posit the 'ataraxia' of my 'I'; I am already lenient when I make use of language, I am the 'unsayable', 'I merely show myself'. And am I not entitled to the terror of my 'I', which repels all that is human, when I do not allow you to disturb me in my self-enjoyment, just like you with your terror of humanity which labels me an 'unman' when I sin against your catechisms?[22]

Stirner's refusal to be a "human being" is not just some vulgar anti-humanism. It rather represents a deep problem for any philosophical-political framework that abstracts from the singularity of individual existence, sacrificing it to some higher cause, universal category, general rule, or moral duty separate from the individual. Stirner poses the question: *How can I be fully I?* We can translate this as such: *How can I refuse the social mediation of domination?* Against being flattened into an identity, function, role, community, nation, or job, Stirner "just want[s] to be 'I', to despise nature, men and their laws, human society and their love, and cut loose from every general relation, even the one of language, with you."[23] Clumsily, and ahead of his time, Stirner is trying to think through the problem of non-identity, the nadir of subjectivity that breaks with the objective determinations of society.[24]

Rejecting the dialectic of idealism, the determinism of

materialism, and the mysticism of religion, Stirner seeks to understand the self-creation of concrete singularity out of abstract universality. In mundane terms, he wants to know how someone can evade domination by the real abstractions of social customs, economic laws, political rights, moral duties, and religious rules, and instead, become something unique, self-determined, their own. The question for Stirner is not how a unique something can come out of an indefinite nothing, but how can a unique nothing create itself out of indefinite somethings.

Is it possible then to read Stirner "out" of context? This would mean reading him not only at a point in time, but as an interruption *of* time, as someone whose thought defiantly evades its time. To read Stirner this way is to take his thought seriously as a challenge. It means, above all, to honor him by consuming him, and ultimately, desecrating him.

Stirner: Practical Philosophy

How then should one interpret the thought of Max Stirner? As Stirner suggests, one person's thoughts are another person's property: "Your thoughts are *my* thoughts, which I dispose of as I will, and which I strike down unmercifully; they are my property, which I annihilate as I wish."[25] To treat thoughts as *property* here does not mean that they are sacred or inviolable; they are not protected by copyright and law. Rather, for Stirner, in order to treat your thoughts as my property, I *must* violate them, make them my own. This is because Stirner thinks that I can only make something my own by taking it, by using and abusing it in my own way. If I refrain from taking and using something uniquely, then I run the risk of letting it control me, dominate me in its fixity or stability. The capacity to appropriate something as *mine* constitutes my power, and the resistance from others to my doing so constitutes theirs. Property exists only in this "manifestation of force."[26]

Stirner thus challenges the reader: *Do you have the power to appropriate me? Can you make me your own?* If property is only meaningful in relation to our power of appropriation, then to declare Stirner's thought *our property* is to expropriate it for ourselves, and violate its boundaries. Violation is the only possible basis for one's property, but even this is not enough, for it is precisely *unique* violation, *my* violation that justifies me, and *your* violation that justifies yours.

The longer we let Stirner's thoughts stiffen and harden over time, the more enslaved we will become to their *independent power*, their congealed status as alienated property or "aliency" [*fremdentum*] against us.[27] On these terms, to consume Stirner means not only to interpret him through our own framework, but rather to mutate his concepts into ours, to violate them until they "bleed to death."[28] In short, to make his thoughts our own, we need to become their "most irreconcilable enemy."[29]

First violation (reading): Stirner should not be read in a doctrinaire manner, as one who posits a system of concepts which cohere on their own. He is not a metaphysician or a systematic writer. This is Marx's great mistake in reading Stirner: he takes him to be laying out thesis after thesis, building up a system which is internally inconsistent and hence, laughably absurd. Marx's reading is violently flat, atonal. How could he have missed such *voice*, such *performance*? The "first readable book in philosophy that Germany has produced," as Ruge called it, *Der Einzige* is nothing if not flamboyant.[30] Let us then read it performatively as a text that utilizes numerous strategies (deduction, dialectic, etymology, allegory, repetition, shock, syllogism, metaphor, neologism, aphorism) to *show* something in its development, a text which provokes an experience in the reader that can only be drawn out indirectly. This operation of the text is self-reflective, revealing its own holes along the way, making the reader often uncomfortable in reading it. Everyone must therefore write their own version as they read it, scalpel in hand.

Second violation (translating): Stirner's language cannot be taken at face value, it must be interpreted. In this reading, I propose numerous translations of Stirnerisms in order to make sense of what appears senseless. This is the double-sided nature of a consumptive reading, both negating and creating, what Bakunin called "creative destruction" in 1842 and Marx would call "productive consumption" in 1857. "Egoist", for example, does not mean "self-interested" or "selfish", but should rather be translated as "one who acts without cause", "unalienated", "unique", "I", "owner", or "squatter." These seemingly disparate terms express more precisely the content of Stirner's concept than our common-sense intuitions of the word "egoist." Other translations would be reading "property" as expropriation, "ownness" as responsibility, "unique" as non-identical, "union" as commune, and "ego" as void.

Third violation (philosophizing): What kind of book is *Der Einzige*? This question is important, because placing the book in any one category will both sterilize some of its richness and, simultaneously, put it into dialogue with others who can elicit more meaning from it through comparison. The process of sterilization and dialogue is unavoidable, for all texts share some affinities with others. I propose here to situate Stirner in at least three categories: "19th century German Philosophy", "Anarchism", and "Ethics." The first is obvious, the second is controversial, the third seems completely absurd. Is Stirner not the most anti-ethical thinker, the destroyer of all ethical systems, the egoist, the nihilist? Ethics, however, as I use the term here, has nothing to do with moral rules but everything to do with one's orientation to *life*.

As Deleuze reads Spinoza,[31] we can read Stirner: a practical philosopher, one who develops a whole grammar for living which fears no death. Stirner's practical philosophy asks how one can become a unique subject, and answers it in terms of power and enjoyment, a language not at all far from Spinoza. In fact, the history of philosophy needs to be redrawn so that

Stirner's text finds its proper place, side by side with Spinoza's *Ethics*, Nietzsche's *Genealogy*, and Levinas's *Totality and Infinity*. If there was not already such a crowd, Bakunin's *God and the State* would join the fray as well.

Each of these texts, operating in different registers for different purposes, develop a non-moralistic ethics, comprising an atheistic philosophical project that confronts the deep political and historical situation of their day. Whether through geometry, genealogy, phenomenology, dialectic, or political intervention, each text *works* on the subject who reads it in a similar way. These works propose a new relation of the self to the self, a turning of the self around itself, attuned to something new, uniquely comported to it. This "care of the self" as ethical subjectivation is what Foucault rightly spots in Stirner as a reawakening of the theme of *epimeleia heautou* from Hellenistic philosophy, especially from Stoicism.[32] Can Stirner "the nihilistic egoist" be read in the same tradition as Marcus Aurelius and Seneca? Not as nihilist or egoist, but as the practical philosopher who advises to, "Ask yourselves and ask after yourselves—that is *practical* and you know you want very much to be 'practical'."[33] With these violations accomplished, we can finally begin to read Stirner.

Ich hab' Mein Sach' auf Stirner gestellt[34]

I have no interest in egoism, whatever that vague concept signifies, and neither should anyone else who reads Max Stirner. *The Ego and Its Own*, or better, *The Unique and its Property*,[35] has nothing to do with egoism, egos, egology, or the sort. All these words are stand-ins, filler for something non-conceptual, even non-representable. But what is this thing and how can it even be discussed? The ego—*das Ich*, I—is not a "thing" at all to Stirner, but a singular *nothing*. To examine it then requires different terminology and different methods, perhaps even a new ontology.

It would be easy here to charge that we are speaking about

a ghost, an abstraction that has taken on shape and become a specter, an apparition, a spook. To speak of something non-representable, in short, is theology. And is not Stirner's project to destroy theology, to consume all gods and masters, and to annihilate anything beyond me which is above me, anything which determines me? "Stirner's ghost-hunt has produced a ghost above all ghosts: the ego!" so goes the charge of Marx and those who follow.

How does one respond to this accusation? In fact, Stirner *already* responded to this charge in his indispensable reply from 1845, written in response to criticisms of his work by Feuerbach, Bauer, Hess, and Szeliga. Stirner writes (in the third person): "What Stirner *says* is a word, a thought, a concept; what he *means* is neither a word, nor a thought, nor a concept. What he says is not the meaning, and what he means cannot be said."[36] In other words, the actuality of any unique I is not identical with its expression in language or thought; the content exceeds the form, and yet to discuss it requires archaic words and static concepts. The objectification of the *I* into a thing, into an "ego", is thus bound to the form of presentation, to language, and not to the content at hand. It is only by "running against the boundaries of language," as Wittgenstein once said, that Stirner approaches the unthinkable, and wrests some truth from the limits of sense.[37]

Truth, according to Stirner, is that which I can maintain against contradiction, and *untruth* is that which I let slip into contradiction through my own weakness.[38] In holding Stirner close to us, how much truth are we willing to let go? This movement against our own desires to let contradiction seep in at every chance we get is the *opposite* of criticism. This marks the intelligence of Stirner's intervention into his own immediate circle—the young Hegelian "critical critics", the *Free*.[39] Against his own comrades who take criticism (and the belief in criticism) to almost apocalyptic heights,[40] Stirner shows "critique" to be nothing but a game of adolescent power in which the players try to ward off their own impotence by wresting truth from their opponents, consuming it as their own property, and drawing power therein. To the *Free*, if I can slice your theory in half with a criticism—if I can find a contradiction inside you—then my power over you increases, my confidence strengthens, my self-worth enhances. For now, your truth is my truth, your power is my power. This logic of critique is a vulgarized Hegelianism, for the goal is to find negations that can propel forward the movement of history and spirit. Such negations, or criticisms, endlessly run around the track of contradiction and resolution, alienation and reappropriation.

Stirner, on the other hand, runs after his *own* contradictions, his own limits, his own negation. Not for any apocalyptic end or final judgment, but rather to reveal the weakness of the dialectic from which he and others draw their strength. Does this confirm his power or expose his vulnerability? May the dialectic collapse so that *I* may live, he seems to say. Stirner thus uses dialectic for *life*, and when its use is worn out, he discards it. The practice of dissolution and consumption may help clarify this. Stirner seeks to dissolve and consume all fixed ideas, but in order to do so, he must use the language of fixed ideas in the process. In one of his pseudonymous replies to critics, Stirner described this problem in the following way: "Stirner himself has described his book as, in part, a clumsy expression of what he wanted to say. It is the arduous work of the best years of his life, and yet he calls it, in part, 'clumsy'. That is how hard he struggled with a language that was ruined by philosophers, abused by state-, religious- and other believers, and enabled a boundless confusion of ideas."[41] In the process of consuming and dissolving the fixed ideas of philosophy, politics, and religion, Stirner himself has been consumed by his own language, which has already been corrupted by those same fixed ideas he is attempting to dissolve.

If language is the "abode of being," as Heidegger once said, then it is a miserable place to live. But how could one ever escape it? Is not that the ultimate idealist fantasy, to ignore empirical constraints and live beyond the realm of language in the space of pure thought, pure consciousness? By rejecting speculative philosophy and evading the stickiness of language, Stirner can easily be charged with mysticism, a philosophy of private experience and the ineffable. Although he often speaks of the "unutterable" and "unspeakable" nature of his task, he *nevertheless* still names it, and carries through.[42]

In naming his objects, Stirner does not endorse "fixity" or a "principle of stability";[43] he does not produce a "phantomalization", as Derrida writes, or some metaphysical identity.[44] Stirner is not a nominalist, rather he is trying to think through the non-identical, as Adorno might say, the punctum of subjectivity that refuses an objective synthesis, the bare I that breaks with its own mediation. For this is the name of an operation without an operator, a vector of action over a gulf of meaning which we can only properly understand as "nothing" or *I*. The nothingness of that which acts is only *retroactively* understood to be something. For in its self-activity, the I knows itself only in its *currentness* as its properties and capacities, memories and desires, thoughts and sensations. To find "meaning" in our own fleeting lives is to accept the *nothingness* out of which we come and into which we go: the *current of time*, the nothing that dissolves all fixed ideas, egos, and relations.[45]

This nothingness is not to be taken "in the sense of emptiness,"[46] Stirner remarks in his preface, but rather as *that from which and into which creation creates*. The non-empty nothingness thus names a kind of presentation, manifestation, or appearance. "I should show myself, that I should appear," Stirner says. That is all that it can do, show itself, appear—*phainesthai*. Beyond that, it is nothing. "I, this nothing, shall put forth my *creations* from myself."[47] The name of the void from which our subjectivity emerges is called *I* [*Ich*]—badly translated as *ego*. Stirner's *I* does not name the identity of consciousness with itself as self-consciousness, but rather it describes an operation that traverses an abyss. What justifies fixing this activity into a concept at all?

Stirner is struggling here to grasp at a truth that he was not yet able to fully develop: the uniqueness of the nothing, its singularity. As the nothingness into which all else can be consumed and dissolved, the I *stands apart* in its negativity. Hegel describes the I as "pure negativity", as the "tremendous power of the negative; it is the energy of thought, of the pure 'I'."[48] As Badiou says of the *void*, it is different in its indifference.[49] The naming of this nothing is justified philosophically due to its unique ontological status, a uniqueness which is "indomitable" and wrecks all attempts of subsumption.[50] So why call this uniqueness *Ich*, I?

First of all, Stirner does not call it *the* I, but always *my* I. This is what separates him from Fichte, who posits "the I" as the absolute principle which grounds the entire science of knowledge. Stirner criticizes his Fichte thusly: "When Fichte says, 'the I is all,' this seems to harmonize perfectly with my thesis. But it is not that the I *is* all, but the I *destroys* all, and only the self-dissolving I, the never-being I, the—*finite* I is really I. Fichte speaks of the 'absolute' I, but I speak of me, the transitory I."[51] Stirner's I is always *in activity*, transitory, never a principle of justification or axiom of a system; it is not *one*, but only grasped as one due to its uniqueness, or difference from all things. It is both incomplete ("never-being") and excessive ("destroys all"), subtracted from and added to "all" that exists. If the "all" is equivalent to all that can be accounted for by *ontology*, then Stirner's I is not *ontological* in any sense. It is the black hole of ontology, the void that blocks the full accounting of things.

Second, "I" functions as a name for this nothing since it is as "I" that one experiences the world. Not as some generic or absolute I, not as a principle like humanity or spirit, but as *this I* which incessantly consumes—takes in, ingests, swallows—experiences, dissolving their multiplicity into the singularity which only "I" can hold together. Stirner's "I" somewhat resembles Kant's transcendental unity of apperception, the "I think" attached to all my experiences as the condition of possibility for their coherence and unity. Yet, whereas Kant's I unifies experience, Stirner's I dissolves it. This "I" weaves through the manifold of experiences as the process of their dissolution. "I", however, does not name *the* process, but *this* one, *mine*.

By qualifying Stirner's use of the word "I" like this, its purely *functional* character becomes apparent. For if the word "I" named a generic process or an absolute principle, then its use would be justified *in itself*. But its use here describes something unique, or better put, a unique nothing, ungraspable beyond its singularity. The name "I" fills in a gap in our ability to reason, functionally satisfying our need to reflect on our own annihilating subjectivity. Yet this term—I, *Ich,* ego—is stuffed with unnecessary psychological baggage that has no place in Stirner's universe. Since it is purely functional, why retain it at all? In other words, to avoid psychologism, we might as well just call the "I" the *unique one* [*der Einzige*].

This is, of course, exactly what Stirner does. This is not only the title of the book, *Der Einzige und sein Eigentum*, but its entire unfolding. It is the fault of the English-language translators to conflate "unique" and "ego", and it is Stirner's fault to suggest this error by repeatedly using terms like "egoism" and "egoist" to describe his philosophy. One must decide whether or not Stirner is justified in using those terms. Why not use another term, another filler or placemat for the unspeakable? As will be shown, even the "ego" must consume itself, for it too is an abstraction to be dissolved. At certain points in the text, this is more apparent than others. Near the end of his book, for instance, Stirner declares that the idea of an "egoist" is itself an illusion: "The egoist, before whom the humanists shudder, is as much a spook as is the devil: he exists only as a spectre and phantasm in their brain."[52] Is this the same egoist that Stirner lauds so strongly

22

throughout the first half of his text? If so, then why praise the egoist only to slander it later? If it is not, then how does the "real" egoist relate to the fantastical image of the egoist? The problem is that Stirner's *Einzige* or *Ich* is not identical with the concept of "egoist" and yet, from the outside, it necessarily *appears* that way. Stirner makes use of this conceptual double exposure in order to provoke his readers and enemies into questioning their own self-assumptions and political beliefs.

The fundamental ambiguity around which Stirner's text revolves is the self-relation of the I. At different points, the I *posits* itself, *dissolves* itself, *consumes* itself, *creates* itself, *destroys* itself, *enjoys* itself, *swallows* itself, *empowers* itself, *reveals* itself, *uses* itself, *abuses* itself, *owns* itself. For instance, while mocking Bruno Bauer, Stirner writes the following about his own presuppositions:

> I, for my part, start from a presupposition in presupposing *myself*, but my presupposition does not struggle for perfection like 'man struggling for perfection,' but only serves me to enjoy and consume it. I alone consume my presupposition, and exist only in consuming it. But that presupposition is therefore not one at all: since I am the unique, I know nothing of the duality of a presupposing and presupposed I (an 'incomplete' and 'complete' I or human being); but that I consume myself, means only that I am. I do not presuppose myself, because at any moment I just am positing or creating myself in the first place, and only because of this am I, not presupposed but posited, and, again posited only in the moment when I posit myself; that is, I am creator and creature in one.[53]

Stirner's non-dualist account of the self as a practical force of negation shines through here. But what does it mean to "consume my presupposition"? How can I *consume* or *own* myself? To grasp the concept of consumption in Stirner, one must go beyond its economic meaning as the "use of a resource." Consumption rather names the process by which I dissolve the separation between myself and my expressions. To consume is to annihilate the fixity and externality of ideas and things that are products of myself yet stand above me. To "consume myself" is thus to continually negate and recycle my own self-expressions of who I take myself to be. In consuming myself, I change who I am and who others take me to be; I block myself from becoming fixed in an identity. By dissolving the independence of my thoughts and relations, I return them back to my power for free play. This cycle of consumption and production of oneself expresses the logic of use and abuse that Stirner calls *property* [*Eigentum*].

Is there any reason to name this activity *egoist*? In fact, this is Stirner's most fundamental mistake or ambivalence, the identification of *das Ich* and *der Einzige* with *der Egoist*. He might as well have said *Anarchist*, for that would at least correspond to the anarchic, groundlessness of the I. "Anarchist" describes a kind of activity without *arche* or principle, irreducible to a higher concept or generality. Furthermore, it lacks the philosophical confusion of the word "egoist". The problem with the term "anarchist", however, comes from its political vagueness, its self-sacrificing idealism to another cause. Perhaps it is better that Stirner stayed away from this disreputable word after all, along with all other labels. For who needs an identity when one has nothing left to identify?

Notes

1. This view is best articulated by Lawrence Stepelevich. See his "Max Stirner as Hegelian" (1985). Along with Stepelevich's essential articles on Stirner, see also McLellan (1969), Moggach (2006), and Tomba (2013). For German research on Stirner, see Essbach (1982), Laska (2000), Kast (2016), and the journal of the Max-Stirner-Gesellschaft in

Leipzig, archived at http://www.max-stirner-archiv-leipzig. de. For a recent, sympathetic interpretation of Max Stirner as a "dialectical egoist", see Welsh (2010).

2. For more on Stirner's life and background, see the classic biography of Stirner by John Mackay (2005), and the chapter by Leopold in Newman (2011).

3. Derrida, *Specters of Marx* (1994)

4. Derrida, 121

5. The other main text being Friedrich Lange's incredibly famous *The History of Materialism* (1865), from which John Henry Mackay learned of Stirner. It was Mackay who "rediscovered" Stirner in the late 19th century, republishing all his work, writing the only existing biography, and tying him to the anarchist tradition. It was possibly Lange's book — or Hartmann's — from which Nietzsche learned of Stirner as well. See Stepelevich's "The Revival of Max Stirner" (1974) for more details.

6. Jensen (2006), 52

7. See Buber (2002).

8. Deleuze, 161

9. Deleuze, 160

10. Deleuze, 160

11. Deleuze, 161

12. Andrew Koch made this claim in his article "Max Stirner: The Last Hegelian or the First Poststructuralist?" (1997) in the UK journal *Anarchist Studies*, and Saul Newman developed it greatly in *From Bakunin to Lacan* (2001). These theorists see Stirner in the same philosophical family as Derrida, Foucault, Lacan, and Deleuze—a "family" which nonetheless has more differences between them, than similarities. Saul Newman above all has developed this interpretation of Max Stirner into a sophisticated *political* theory of "postanarchism," for instance, in *The Politics of Postanarchism* (2010) and *Postanarchism* (2016). Newman

has also been central in reigniting academic interest in Max Stirner within the English-speaking world. See his fantastic edited collection *Max Stirner* (2011), published by Palgrave Macmillan.

13. Arvon (1954)

14. Mackay (2005), Tucker (2005), Clark (1976)

15. Heider (1994)

16. Helms (1966)

17. Carroll (1974)

18. EO, 35

19. EO, 301

20. EO, 7

21. EO, 159. See also: 112, 121, 124, 125, 130–1, 159, 161, 219, 239, 256, 296, 309, 318.

22. G. Edward [Max Stirner], "The Philosophical Reactionaries" (1847), translated by W. De Ridder in: *Max Stirner*, ed. Newman (2011), 103

23. *Ibid.*

24. On the problem of non-identity, see Adorno, *Negative Dialectics* (1973).

25. EO, 302

26. EO, 289

27. EO, 279. I will come back to this neologism of Stirner.

28. EO, 252

29. EO, 58. In Stirner's framework, the strongest enemy of something is also the owner of it. For only as enemy of that which I own can I preempt any other enemies of mine.

30. Arnold Ruge, letter to his mother, December 17, 1844. Cited in EO, Leopold's intro, xiii.

31. See Deleuze, *Spinoza: Practical Philosophy* (1988).

32. See Foucault's 1981–1982 Lectures at the College de France published in 2005 in English as *The Hermeneutics of the Subject*. The reference to Stirner is on page 251.

33. EO, 146

34. "All things are Stirner to me". More literally: I have set my affair on Stirner.

35. The standard French and Spanish translations, for instance, are much closer to the German original. The choice to translate *"Einzige"* (unique one) as *Ego* was made by Benjamin R. Tucker, the American individualist anarchist who funded and published the English translation of Stirner by Steven T. Byington.

36. *Stirner's Critics* (2012), 55, translated by Wolfi Landstreicher. See also the fantastically partisan introduction by Jason McQuinn. For the German, see *Parerga, Kritiken, Repliken* (1986) edited by Laska. Stirner's replies to his critics are *essential reading* for anyone interested in Stirner. They clear up mountains of confusion, especially concerning his views on "egoism", the "unique", and the "un-man."

37. See Wittgenstein (1965).

38. EO, 312. But see also, 263–265, 303–315.

39. For background on *The Free*, see Mackay (2005), McLellan (1969), and Stepelevich (1983).

40. For background, see Eric Luft's essay "Edgar Bauer and the Origins of the Theory of Terrorism" in *The New Hegelians*, ed. Moggach (2006).

41. G. Edward [Max Stirner], "The Philosophical Reactionaries" in: *Max Stirner*, ed. Newman (2011), 114

42. "Only thoughtlessness really saves me from thoughts. It is not thinking, but my thoughtlessness, or I the unthinkable, incomprehensible, that frees me from possession." EO, 133

43. EO 271 on "fixity", EO 298 on "principle of stability." The Hegelian influence on this critique of "fixity" will be explored later.

44. "The history of the ghost remains a history of phantomalization..." Derrida, 123

45. "It is different if you do not chase after an *ideal* as your 'destiny' but dissolve yourself as time dissolves everything.

The dissolution is not your destiny because it is current [*Gegenwart*]." EO, 294

46. EO, 7

47. EO, 209

48. Hegel, *Phenomenology of Spirit* (1977), §22 and §32. See also §37: "That is why some of the ancients conceived the *void* as the principle of motion, for they rightly saw the moving principle as the *negative*, though they did not as yet grasp that the negative is the self."

49. See Badiou, *Being and Event* (2006), Meditations 4 and 5, where this point is developed.

50. "Exertions to 'form' all men into moral, rational, pious, human, 'beings' (that is, training), have been in vogue from time immemorial. They are wrecked against the indomitable quality of I, against own nature, against egoism." EO, 294

51. EO, 163

52. EO, 317

53. EO, 135

Part II: Stirner's World

The structure of *Der Einzige und sein Eigentum* looks like this:

All Things are Nothing to Me[1] [*Ich hab' Mein' Sach' auf Nichts gestellt*]

First Part: *Man* [*Der Mensch*]

I. A Human Life [*Ein Menschenleben*]

II. Men of Ancient and Modern Times [*Menschen der alten und neuen Zeit*]

1. The Ancients [*Die Alten*]

2. The Moderns [*Die Neuen*]

§1. The Spirit [*Der Geist*]

§2. The Possessed [*Die Besessenen*]

§3. The Hierarchy [*Die Hierarchie*]

3. The Free [*Die Freien*]

§1. Political Liberalism [*Der politische Liberalismus*]

§2. Social Liberalism [*Der soziale Liberalismus*]

§3. Humane Liberalism [*Der humane Liberalismus*]

Second Part: *I* [*Ich*]

I. Ownness [*Die Eigenheit*]

II. The Owner [*Der Eigner*]

1. My Power [*Meine Macht*]

2. My Intercourse [*Mein Verkehr*]

3. My Self-Enjoyment [*Mein Selbstgenuss*]

III. The Unique One [*Der Einzige*]

Stirner is clearly targeting Feuerbach in the very division of parts one and two. Whereas Feuerbach's 1841 bombshell, *The Essence of Christianity,* splits into *God* and *Man*, Stirner's work divides into *Man* and *I*. Feuerbach's secularization of Hegel ends up elevating the category of Man; Stirner's demystification of Man elevates only I. The formal similarity masks significant qualitative differences. The idea of *God*, for Feuerbach, turns out to be only the projection and absolutization of the essence of man, which is grasped through the unity of reason, love and will; theology, in other words, becomes anthropology. But *Man* or *Humanity* for Stirner has nothing to do with the essence of I. Whether theological or anthropological, *any* positing of an "essence" as such is doomed, "wrecked against the indomitable quality of I."[2] *Man* is not the alienated expression of the essence of I, but the alienation of only one of its properties. Such properties can never exhaust me, their owner, and no matter how necessary, contingent, broad or narrow they may be, they are all qualitatively the same in relation to my I: they are my *property*, and hence, disposable.

The first half of *Der Einzige* exhibits many failed attempts at positing an essence of the *I*. Stirner's position is that no matter how far (God) or close (man), how honorable (freedom) or righteous (justice), how abstract (truth) or material (labor), *any separation* of myself from myself which would determine me *as such* is categorically equivalent: it is absolutely other—alien. For Stirner, the category of man or human being (*Mensch*) is not sublated by I; it is not resolved, understood, fixed, or reformed. The humanity of "Man" is annihilated by the I which annihilates itself along with it. Even the category of the "world" is not safe, for as Stirner remarks, "I *annihilate it* as I annihilate myself; I *dissolve it*."[3]

Stirner was no philosophical dilettante. He was indeed quite familiar with Hegel's philosophy, having been the only young Hegelian (besides Feuerbach) to have seen him lecture in Berlin.[4] Hegel's influence over Stirner is strong, and present. This can be seen by merely looking at the triplets and sub-triplets that make up the structure of his book, similar to Hegel's triplet and sub-triplet (and sub-sub-triplet) structure in the *Science of Logic*. The syllogistic structure of Hegel's dialectical method (i.e., the self-negating movement of universal, particular, and individual) grounds this practice, and we see it all over Stirner.

The beginning and ending of Stirner's book are both unique, not only in their brevity but in their comprehensive aim. Both are sealed with the declaration of "nothing", and both aim at justifying the *Einzige* as the only one capable of grasping this. "All things are nothing to me... The Unique One" — it is between these two points that the drama unfolds.

Stirner's Logic

The first half of *Der Einzige* tells the same story in different guises, different triplets, different allegories. No matter the setting or characters, what is repeatedly iterated across psychological, sociological, historical, and philosophical planes is the story of how an idea or relation becomes a thing, and either a) how that thing becomes more real than the thinker who thought it in the first place or b) how the relations between individuals become separate from the individuals themselves. Once this thing is "fixed", it almost gravitationally pulls individuals into a more general "subjection", one which empties their uniqueness and individuality out of them, replacing it with the staleness of a generalized equivalent, a "generality" [*Allgemeinheit*].[5] The general equivalent is the ideological chain that binds the individual to the coherence of the social whole; it is the "cement" of society and the state.[6]

In relation to *ideas*, the inversion of subject and object occurs when a thought, as generality, is elevated and sanctified, thus flattering the individual. The consecration of thought, according to Stirner, degrades and abases the individual into a position of submission to that sacred object. "*Everything sacred is a tie, a fetter.*"[7] Flattered by the exaltation of one's ideas beyond oneself, one willingly submits to its new form as "ruling principle."[8] This structure reveals itself as "the meaning of hierarchy", or the "dominion of thoughts."[9] Such dominion is only accomplished with the total eradication of individuality and uniqueness.[10] Only the *unique one* is capable of puncturing the generality of the sacred tie, thus rupturing the stability of the social whole. Because of this threat, any incommensurable difference, i.e., the singularity of a unique individual, must be either outlawed, killed, or colonized. One who wants to maintain their individuality within this order must necessarily become an enemy, a criminal, a *desecrator* — all laudable categories for Stirner. "The individual is the irreconcilable enemy of every *generality*, every *tie*, every fetter."[11] "Nothing is holy to him."[12] "An own I cannot desist from being a criminal, that crime is his life."[13] More than that, one might have to bring down an empire in order to raise oneself up. This requires one to become a "perverter of law" [*Rechtsverdreher*] — like Alcibiades, Lysander, Christ, and Luther — for "everything sacred is and must be perverted by perverters of the law."[14]

How could the inversion of *thinking* and *thought* lead to the downfall of empires? This sounds suspiciously idealist. The problem is that the dialectic of thinker/thought/thing is too narrow to account for what Stirner seeks; the content exceeds the form, and hence the form should be revised. The previous formula did not consider the actual meaning of the relations between such categories. Stirner interprets this relation through a mutilated dialectical grid stitched to an inverted Proudhonian view of property. This process of subjection can be better formalized as the relation between an owner and property in which the property transforms into something alien to the owner, an "aliency" [*Fremdentum*].[15] The thinker is just one type of owner, the thought is just one kind of property, and the generality, sacred tie, and ruling principle are manifestations of the same logic of alienation. The owner and their property are bound to each other such that the property is determined by the power of the owner. It can be formalized like this: *Owner(property)* — i.e., property is dependent on the owner. Crucial here is the fact that the property at hand does not *exhaust* the individuality of the owner, their unicity. Alienation occurs when the dependency relation is broken, when property becomes independent of the owner's power. It can be written like this: *Property(owner)* — i.e., the owner is now defined by its relation to the property. This form of property determines the owner, yet it is not determined by the owner. However, the property is still the property *of the owner*. When one's own property becomes independent of one's own power, it is alienated property or *alienty*. This can be formulated as such:

A. [Owner(property)→Property(owner)]→Alienty

This symbolizes the domination of one's property over and through the owner itself.

It is important to note that this phenomenon does not define or express *all* human relations, nor is it universally valid for all times. Human beings are engaged and entangled in innumerable projects with their manifold desires, and in no way are they just thinking, positing, owning, submitting, resisting beings. To Stirner, before we are idealist youths searching for essences behind things, we are realistic children playing with things as they appear. Growing up, for Stirner, is precisely the loss of "realism" and the descent into "idealism", which can only be overcome by "egoism."[16]

Stirner's quasi-dialectic of alienation has three moments: *Owning*, *Alienating*, and *Reifying*. Owned property (one's power over an idea, relation, thing, x) becomes alienated from its creator (inversion of subject and object), and, ultimately, reified into an objective thing (independence of the object from oneself). In the first two moments, the owner and the property are still defined in terms of each other; in the third moment, however, a separate essence is granted to the property *in itself*. Reification is the proper term for the final moment, since it is a modification of alienation in which the separation of the property from the owner leads one to treat it as an independent thing, with its own self-determined meaning and power. The "seeming-body" [*Scheinleib*] of property thus becomes an actual body.[17] This process can be formalized like this:

B. $[x(y) \rightarrow y(x)] \rightarrow z$

Stirner populates this formula with different terms and concepts. For x, he uses *self, I, corporeal, thing,* and *creator*; for y, *spirit, own, ghost, idea, creature*; for z, *specter (spook), alien, corporeal ghost, fixed idea,* and *creator* again. They can be written as such:

C. $[Self(spirit) \rightarrow Spirit(self)] \rightarrow Specter (spook)$
D. $[I(own) \rightarrow Own(I)] \rightarrow Alien$
E. $[Corporeal(ghost) \rightarrow Ghost(corporeal)] \rightarrow Corporeal ghost$
F. $[Thing(idea) \rightarrow Idea(thing)] \rightarrow Fixed Idea$
G. $[Creator(creature) \rightarrow Creature(creator)] \rightarrow Creator$

For all the venom Marx spewed on Stirner, he used a similar logic in *Capital* when describing the fetish character of the commodity. For Marx, labor under conditions of capitalism is both concrete and abstract, and the value of the commodity one produces requires a specific form in which to express itself. Ultimately, for Marx, this form is money, and its power obscures the social relations which produce value, leading human beings to treat it as the agent itself. In other words, my labor produces a commodity whose 'value' I treat separately from my own activity. It becomes a fetish, dominating me in turn.[18] Thus:

H. $[Labor(commodity) \rightarrow Commodity(labor)] \rightarrow Commodity$-Fetish

Is reification a necessary consequence of alienation, or is there some room for contingency between the two? In other words, can property become alienated without necessarily leading to its independent power? It would seem at least intuitively possible that this could occur. For example, I can grant the idea of love dominance over me, while still maintaining that love is, in the end, still *my* idea. For Stirner, any break in my control over property opens the door to its domination over me. Whether or not this is necessary, the very possibility is dangerous enough to warrant its indiscriminate foreclosure. With that said, *any and every* relation to property is necessarily ambiguous, for it is both something I seek for my consumption and something I fight against for my own independence.

Stirner's Allegories

Given this background, where does Stirner begin his analysis? From this subject, I, that which I call *my own*: the living, actual individual being that I am. What exactly constitutes the "actuality" of this corporeal being is purposely left undetermined, for to fix it in any way would open up the door to the problem that Stirner is explicitly trying to avoid: the problem of essence. But by leaving it so vague, he allows Marx and others to charge that it is not "actual" actuality that characterizes this being but ideal actuality, actuality seen from the standpoint of thought. In *The German Ideology*, Marx makes this accusation: "This 'I' of Stirner's which is the final outcome of the hitherto existing world is, therefore, not a 'corporeal individual' but a category constructed on the Hegelian method."[19] The *true* standpoint, according to Marx, is to see the "I" from the perspective of "living, material labor." And since living, material labor is *more actual* than this individual "creative nothing" that Stirner describes, we must reject Stirner as all too metaphysical. The accusation of being "too metaphysical", which plagued much of 20th century philosophy, can be seen *in nuce* right there in Marx's early polemic with Stirner.

What, then, is this I? As individual and corporeal, finite and intentional, it thinks, desires, and acts. Most importantly, it has the capacity to be self-determining, as well as to be determined by others. One property of this "I" is its ability to think and create thought-entities, immaterial realities, spirits. Let's call these objects "x." Now some of these thought-things can become separated from this I, and hold power over it, such as God, the good, truth, humanity, justice, nation, and freedom.[20] Let's call these special thought-things X. X names a spiritual idea that becomes so exalted as to determine the nature of the I. The basic structure for this process was laid out in formulas A and B. To restate it here with these new terms: $[I(x) \rightarrow X(I)] \rightarrow X$.

How does this work in reality? In Part I of *The Ego and Its Own*, Stirner gives four different accounts of how this logic of separation unfolds. They are outlined in terms of developmental psychology, philosophy, history, and politics. Now these accounts are provocative at best, racist and specious at worst. All these sequences, except the political one, are appropriated from Hegel's lectures on history and philosophy, which Stirner knew quite well. Stirner organized them in a tri-partite sequence instead of a quadratic scheme, probably because he thought it was more dialectical.[21] The first three—psychology, philosophy, and history—place "our" time within the center term, on the cusp between it and the next term, the future to come. In Stirner's framework, we are currently youthful, idealist, mongoloid, Christians in the process of becoming adult, egoist, Caucasian atheists. The first category represents our dependence on the things of material world, the middle moment expresses the dominance of mind, ideas and spirit, whereas the third is the future of the self-owning I.[22]

What is Stirner doing here exactly? At face value, these stories are laughable and offensive. And not only that, but "copied" from Hegel, as Marx repeatedly complains. They do not quite match the earlier logic outlined, although there is similarity in the number of terms used. More properly dialectical, each moment here is a negation of the previous one. Given these facts, what should we do with them? As empirical "proofs" of his theory, we should obviously reject them, not only because they are wrong, but also because they are idiotic and racist. But are they meant to be empirically accurate? One should rather ask another question: What is Stirner's relation to the material he is presenting? Is it serious or parody? The material is obviously not his own, but who owns history, anyway? Who has the right to use and abuse a theory? They are not his "property" per se, but they are the "material" from which his thinking occurs. Here one needs to look at how Stirner thinks one should relate to other people's property. In one of his critiques of the liberal theory of property—property as a sacred, inviolable right—he asserts his position on the page, loud and clear: "I do not shyly step back from your property, but look upon it always as *my* property, in which I need to 'respect' nothing. Pray do the same with what you call my property."[23]

If we read Stirner as he asks to be read, as someone making his *own* property out of whatever material is in his power to consume, then we should read the aforementioned cases as nothing but *allegories* for his underlying purpose. Making property out of something else, appropriating it, making sense of it to oneself and for oneself—that is what Stirner does. To make sense of the material he is given, he manipulates certain symbols into recognizable forms within his own language; he allegorizes and parodies.

Stirner's purpose is to dislodge fixed ideas *by any means necessary*. Where does this desire to demolish such fixity arise from? If we consider Stirner as still Hegelian, then we can see him as following through on Hegel's call to liberate thinking from its fixity. In the *Phenomenology of Spirit*, Hegel describes this modern task of philosophy:

Hence the task nowadays consists not so much in purging the individual of an immediate, sensuous mode of apprehension, and making him into a substance that is an object of thought and that thinks, but rather in just the opposite, in *freeing determinate thoughts from their fixity* so as to give actuality to the universal, and impart to it a spiritual life.[24]

Stirner recognizes this, and has his work cut out for him, since the fixity of thought does not simply go away. Fixed ideas are deceptive because their presence is itself denied by those who possess them. One could say that such people are in *bad faith*, self-deceived, possessed. And we all know that "possessed [*Besessene*] people are *set* [*versessen*] in their opinions."[25] If that is the case, then a simple injunction to abolish them is not enough. One has to first bring them to the surface, to make them *present* and not merely spectral. Like the analyst does for the analysand, one must *conjure* them, make them *conscious* to the bearer, so that they can be recognized in thought and reabsorbed in practice.

Conjuring tricks! — the materialist philosopher cries. *Where is the history, empiricity?* This question, however, misses the motivation and goal for the conjuring; it ignores the ethical drive. People must first realize the ghosts or fixed ideas at work in order to expose the "wheels in the head".[26] Second, if the goal is to exorcise ghosts, to abolish them, reappropriate, consume, and dissolve them, then who cares how we get there? By facts or affects, nothing should be precluded. To break through the veil of bad faith and expose the spooks for what they are, Stirner tells a story about how they appeared in the first place, the story of *subjection*. He gives an account of how and why it is that "subjects vegetate in subjection".[27] This is the reason for his reappropriation of Hegel's historical schemas: they are not dialectical *per se*, but rather allegories of dialectical transitions, parodies of "historical" thinking in which the present is always the best outcome of the past. This seems to be the only way to justify their presence.

The only real creativity that Stirner shows in terms of the

allegories is the last one, still relevant today: the so-called 'dialectic' of liberalism. It can be formulated as such:

Political Liberalism→Social Liberalism (Communism) →Humane Liberalism (Humanism, Criticism)

This section, following the ancients and the moderns, is called "The Free." Named after the group of Stirner's proto-Bohemian, intellectual, revolutionary, young Hegelian comrades in Berlin (of whom Marx, Engels, Ruge, and Bruno Bauer were fellow travelers at one point or another), Stirner's attack was directed towards them, a gift they must have truly enjoyed. The "Free" are not *distinct* from the moderns, but are rather only the "more modern and most modern among the 'moderns' and are put in a separate division merely because they belong to the present, and what is present, above all, claims our attention here."[28] This theoretical move is similar to what a century and a half later would happen with the term "postmodern" — that which is not beyond the modern, but only the most contemporary form of modernity, the present.[29]

Another difference with this sequence is that all the terms of the triad already exist, in fact, they coexist in the present. There is no resolution in the final term, no future reconciliation to come. Political, social and humane liberalism are all plagued by the same error, and only their entire dissolution will get us beyond them. Political liberalism is tied to the republicanism of the French Revolution (e.g., Rousseau, Kant, Robespierre); social liberalism is Stirner's phrase for the new ideologies of socialism and communism (that is, *before* Marx, more related to Proudhon and the utopian socialism of Weitling); finally, humane liberalism is the name Stirner gives to the "critical criticism" of the young Hegelians, especially their form of secular critique which elevates man while lowering God and state (e.g., Feuerbach, Bauer). Remarkable about this political topography is that all three views are not only present, but still influential today. Political liberalism has been renamed "democracy", and is the key banner around which most political claims are justified; social liberalism, or socialism, still animates the desire for alternatives to capitalism; and humane liberalism, or humanism, is the basic framework for international human rights law and discourse.

Political liberalism seeks a free state where citizens unite together as a nation under the ideal of political freedom.[30] The overthrow of absolute monarchy, the installing of a sovereign republic, the granting of inalienable rights—these are its tropes. Freedom from arbitrary masters—that is its cry. This theory posits a social contract in which individuals agree to give up their power to an authoritative body that governs through representation and is bound by *law*. Although a republic can be brought about by revolution, the end result is by no means revolutionary. As Stirner argues, "The revolution was not directed against *the established*, but against the *establishment in question*, against a *particular* establishment. It did away with *this* ruler, not with *the* ruler."[31] This new ruler or "mundane god"—the state—bestows political liberty on its subjects.[32] But as Stirner will later claim, freedom can never be given, only *taken*.[33] Political liberalism fools us into thinking that freedom is a *gift*. With spite and flare, Stirner indicts this fantasy:

'Political freedom', what are we to understand by this? Perhaps the individual's freedom *from* the state and its laws? No; on the contrary, the individual's *bondage* in the state and to the state's laws. But why 'freedom'? Because one is no longer separated from the state by intermediaries, but stands in direct and immediate relation to it; because one is a—citizen, not the subject of another... Political freedom, this fundamental doctrine of liberalism, is nothing but a second phase of—Protestantism... Political freedom means that the *polis*, the state, is free; freedom of religion that religion is free, as freedom of conscience signifies that conscience is free; not, therefore, that I am free from the state, from religion, from conscience, or that I am *rid* of them. It does not mean *my* freedom, but the freedom of a power that rules and subjugates me; it means that one of my *oppressors*, like state, religion, conscience, is free. State, religion, conscience, these oppressors, make me a slave, and *their* freedom is *my* slavery.[34]

At first glance, Stirner's critique of political freedom resembles Marx's criticism of political emancipation from his essay, *On the Jewish Question*, published the same year, and definitely read by Stirner.[35] For both, the "political" sphere does not liberate me but rather separates me from my own particularity, splitting me into a public "citizen" and a private "bourgeois." In the state, I am only a citizen, never my concrete self, with needs, desires, and interests. For Marx, the state is the alienated social power of human beings. For Stirner, however, the freedom of the state does not derive from some abstraction called "human species-being", but from *me*, and the more freedom the state has, the less do I.

Social liberalism pierces through this veneer of freedom, but goes no farther in rectifying it. In the state of political liberalism, people are all equally "free" in relation to the law (i.e., free from arbitrary masters), but they are not equally free in terms of other aspects of their life, like property or wealth. Although "persons have become *equal*, their *possessions* have not."[36] This disparity of possessions creates a new kind of subjection, *class* domination. For Stirner, such material inequality creates a system of mutual dependency: "The poor *need the rich*, the rich the poor, the former the rich man's money, the latter the poor man's labor. So no one needs another as a *person*, but as a *giver*, and thus as one who has something to give, as holder or possessor. So what he *has*, makes the *man*. And in *having*, or in 'possessions,' people are unequal."[37]

The social inequality of individuals in a bourgeois state is not due to greed or chance, according to Stirner, but to the basic framework of political liberalism which disregards material possessions when formally accounting for equal freedom before the law. The poor and the rich are unequally dependent on each other *not* as citizens of right, but as sellers and buyers of possessions, whether that be labor or money. In such a system, the vast majority of individuals are forced to work for others in order to satisfy their needs. Such labor—even in a 'free' society—is nothing but a modification of slavery. Stirner uses Adam Smith's classic pin factory example, as did Hegel, in order to emphasize how workers are subjugated through their own alienated activity:

> Condemning a man to machine-like labor amounts to the same thing as slavery. If a factory worker must tire himself to death twelve hours and more, he is cut off from becoming a human being... He who in a pin-factory only puts on the heads, only draws the wire, works, as it were, mechanically, like a machine... his labor cannot *satisfy* him, it can only *fatigue* him. His labor is nothing by itself, has no object *in itself*, is nothing complete in itself; he labors only into another's hands, and is *used* (exploited) by this other.[38]

Used and exploited by another, cut off from becoming fully human, performing deadening machine-like work—Stirner's descriptions are eerily close to Marx's 1844 Paris manuscripts, unpublished at the time. This makes sense, since both were reading the same sources and listening to the same communist criticisms. For Stirner, however, these communists criticize the unfreedom, inequality and alienation of bourgeois society from a deficient standpoint: the standpoint of labor.[39] Recognizing the lies of the bourgeoisie, communists posit *labor* as the new ground of equality. The standpoint of labor thus becomes the *standpoint* of critique, and not the *object* of critique: "This is our equality, or herein we are *equal*, in that we, I as well as you, and you and all of you, are active or 'labor' each one for the rest; in that each of us is a *worker*... It is *labor* that constitutes our dignity and our—equality... Labor is our sole value all the same: that we are *workers* is the best thing about us... All workers (workers, of course, in the sense of workers 'for the common good', that is, communistic workers) are equal."[40]

The critique of exploitation and the unmasking of inequality are both positive developments, but they turn problematic once *labor* is taken to be the "new" essence of man. To Stirner, individuals are always more than any one of their particular properties, including the property of labor-power. Labor-power may be a necessary condition of existence, but its elevation into metaphysical status negates one's other properties and powers. The identification of the essence of human beings with their ability to work is thus to mistake the historically specific, functional reduction of individuals to mere labor-power in capitalism with a timeless thesis of philosophical anthropology. This critique of the standpoint of labor, written four years before the *Communist Manifesto* of Marx and Engels, is now considered a contemporary development.[41] Both in this criticism and in his only direct reference to Marx (in which he criticizes the concept of *species-being*), Stirner is then already our contemporary.[42]

The second fault in the communist perspective occurs at the level of political strategy. If possessions are what make people unequal, then an equalizing measure would be to abolish all possessions. *No more private property!* Where would the property go? Since our intrinsic equality lies in our labor, and since all labor is inherently social, all property should go to *society*. Society displaces the state as the fundamental sovereign, becoming that by which equality and freedom is recognized, and that from which authority and rights are granted. Another *change of masters*, Stirner notes, another wheel in the head. "Society, from which we have everything, is a new master, a new spook, a new 'supreme being', which 'takes us into its service and duty!'"[43] Giving all our property to a new master makes us neither free nor equal, but precisely *propertyless*. "Let us then do away with *personal property*. Let no one have anything any longer, let every one be a—bum [*Lump*]. Let property be *impersonal*, let it belong to—*society*."[44] In bourgeois society, we at least have some property to cushion our subjection; in this version of "communism", we would not even have that.

With political liberalism, freedom was based on the equal subjection of everyone to the law. With social liberalism, freedom was based on the equal reduction of all to their status as workers. With humane liberalism, the third and final political ideology that Stirner criticizes, freedom is based on the universal humanity of man. Humane liberalism, or humanism, is the movement to *humanize* all aspects of life, to make life more humane. We are all *human beings*, and so our humanity should be the criteria for all things.

If communism was right in wanting to change the exploitation of labor, it did not go far enough in terms of the actual *content* of labor. Factory labor, farm labor, service work—these are all done only for the end result, the wage. The point of such work is leisure, escape. This is *too egoistical*, the humanists proclaim, this is only a "worker's consciousness [*Arbeiter-bewusstsein*]."[45] Instead, we need humanist labor and a humane consciousness. What is the basis of our humanity, according to this view? Self-consciousness, the ability to reason and think: "The restless mind is the true laborer."[46] No prejudice shall be unquestioned, no object unexamined, no limit respected. "The humane liberal wants that labor of the *mind* which *works up* all material; he wants the mind, that leaves no thing quiet or in its existing condition, that acquiesces in nothing, analyses everything, criticizes anew every result that has been gained."[47] The critical, reasoning mind becomes the new criteria for humanity. Labor is no longer to be done for egoistical ends, but for the sake of progress and humanity.

But I am not just human, Stirner responds, I am *un-human*. Humanity is merely one of my properties, it does not define *me*, rule me. In fact, no one is a generic human being, "only the *un-man* is an *actual* human being."[48] To flip an old saying, *everything human is alien to me*:

> Human beings that are not human beings, what should they be but *ghosts*? Every actual human being, because he does not correspond to the concept 'human being', or because he is not a 'generic human being', is a spook. But do I still remain an un-man even if I reduced humanity—which towered above me and remained other-worldly to me only as my ideal, my task, my essence or concept—to my own inherent *property* in me; so that the human being is nothing else than my humanity, my human existence, and everything that I do is human precisely because I do it, but not because it corresponds to the concept 'human being'? *I* am actually human and un-human in one; for I am human and at the same time more than human; I am I of this, my mere property.[49]

Humane liberalism accomplishes what political and social liberalism began: the eradication of individuality. First, individual authority was displaced onto the state as law; then, individual property was given to society through labor; now, individual self-determination is given to humanity through reason. The end result is a generic working, thinking, human citizen; that is what I must be in order to count in society, to be a part of the whole. Without these basic conditions met, I do not even exist. Together, they let me appear and grant me freedom.

This freedom, however, is not *mine*, since it is based on

renouncing myself. For Stirner, anything which fixes me in a single identity, property, or essence can never make me free. Political liberalism, rooted in political liberty, made the state free. Social liberalism, grounded in the desire for social equality, made society free. Humane liberalism, seeking a world of human equality, made humanity free. State, society, humanity—*a change of masters*. What we give up in all cases is our *ownness*, the power to uniquely determine our own non-identity. *Egoists!*—the liberals shout. But that too is their spook.

Notes

1. A more literal translation of this central phrase would be "I have set my affair on nothing" or "I have based my cause on nothing." However, the more lyrical "All things are nothing to me" better expresses Stirner's meaning, which is that nothing alien should rule me—whether that be a cause, concern, affair, object, relation, idea, or anything at all.
2. EO, 294
3. EO, 262
4. See Stepelevich, "Max Stirner as Hegelian" (1985).
5. EO, 192. *Allgemeinheit* can also be translated as "universality", which would fit better with Hegel. However, I stick to the standard translation here to emphasize Stirner's unique use of the term.
6. EO, 212: "By this cement [law] the total of the state is held together." Without it: "... anarchy and lawlessness."
7. EO, 192
8. EO, 59: "A fixed idea may also be perceived as 'maxim', 'principle', 'standpoint' and the like." See also EO, 200: "the state is the *ruling principle*."
9. EO, 68
10. This statement sounds extreme, but only if one reads it as implying that such dominion has been completely accomplished. For Stirner, that is impossible.

11. *"Alles Heilige ist ein Band, eine Fessel."* EO, 192
12. EO, 165
13. EO, 181
14. For Alcibiades, Lysander, Luther, see EO, 190–192. For Christ "the insurgent", see EO, 280–281. For "perverters of the law", see EO, 192.
15. Stirner criticizes Proudhon's theory of property for being too "compassionate", since he blames others for robbing us, instead of faulting us for not robbing the rich. Stirner concludes that the real problem is not property as such, but propertylessness, or its alienation: "In general, no one grows indignant at *his*, but at *alien* property. They do not in truth attack property, but the alienation of property. They want to be able to call *more*, not less, *theirs*; they want to call everything *theirs*. They are fighting, therefore, against *alienness* [*Fremdheit*], or, to form a word similar to property [*Eigentum*], against alienty [*Fremdentum*]." EO, 279
16. See EO, Part I, "A Human Life," 13–18, where Stirner outlines the psychological development of human beings in three stages: the realist child, the idealist youth, and the egoist adult. This life sequence was appropriated from Hegel, e.g. §396 of Hegel's *Philosophy of Mind* (1971). On the similarities and differences between Hegel and Stirner's developmental schemas, see Stepelevich, "Ein Menschenleben: Hegel and Stirner" in Moggach, *The New Hegelians* (2006), 166–175.
17. EO, 36: "Yes, the whole world is haunted! Only *is* haunted? Indeed, it itself haunts, it is uncanny through and through, it is the wandering seeming-body [*Scheinleib*] of a spirit, it is a spook. What else is a ghost other than an apparent body, but a real spirit? Well, the world is 'vain,' is 'nothing', is only dazzling 'semblance' [*Schein*]; its truth is only the spirit; it is the seeming-body of a spirit."
18. See Marx, *Capital*, Volume I, Chapter 1, Section 4, MECW 35.
19. Marx and Engels, *The German Ideology*, MECW 5: 192

20. See the opening to *Der Einzige*: "What is not supposed to be my concern! First and foremost the good cause, then God's cause, the cause of mankind, of truth, of freedom, of humanity, of justice; further, the cause of my people, my prince, my fatherland; finally, even the cause of mind and a thousand other causes. Only my cause is never to be my concern." EO, 5

21. August von Cieszkowski, an even earlier young Hegelian critic, already did this in his *Prolegomena Zur Historiosophie* (1838), partially translated in *The Young Hegelians: An Anthology*, ed. Stepelevich.

22. On psychology, EO 13–18; on philosophy, EO 19–62; on history, EO 62–89; on politics, EO 89–135.

23. EO, 220

24. Hegel (1977), *Phenomenology of Spirit*, paragraph 33, page 19–20, italics mine. Here is the full quote: "In modern times, however, the individual finds the abstract form ready-made; the effort to grasp and appropriate it is more the direct driving-forth of what is within and the truncated generation of the universal than it is the emergence of the latter from the concrete variety of existence. Hence the task nowadays consists not so much in purging the individual of an immediate, sensuous mode of apprehension, and making him into a substance that is an object of thought and that thinks, but rather in just the opposite, in freeing determinate thoughts from their fixity so as to give actuality to the universal, and impart to it a spiritual life. But it is far harder to bring fixed thoughts into a fluid state than to do so with sensuous existence. The reason for this was given above: fixed thoughts have the 'I', the power of the negative, or pure actuality, for the substance and element of their existence, whereas sensuous determinations have only powerless, abstract immediacy, or being as such. Thoughts become fluid when pure thinking, this inner *immediacy*,

recognizes itself as a moment, or when the pure certainty of self abstracts from itself—not by leaving itself out, or setting itself aside, but by giving up the *fixity* of its self-positing, by giving up not only the fixity of the pure concrete, which the 'I' itself is, in contract with its differentiated content, but also the fixity of the differentiated moments which, posited in the element of pure thinking, share the unconditioned nature of the 'I'. Through this movement the pure thoughts become *Notions*, and are only now what they are in truth, self-movements, circles, spiritual essences, which is what their substance is." Hegel (1977), 19–20

25. EO, 44
26. EO, 43. "Wheels in the head" loosely translates the German idiom "*Sparren zu viel haben.*" It can also be: "you have a screw loose", or plainly, "you are crazy."
27. EO, 44
28. EO, 89
29. See, for instance, David Harvey's *The Condition of Postmodernity* (1989) or Fredric Jameson's *Postmodernism, or, The Cultural Logic of Late Capitalism* (1991).
30. See EO, 90: "Let us then hold together and protect the human being in each other; then we find the necessary protection in our *holding together* [*Zusammenhalt*], and in ourselves, *those who hold together* [*Zusammenhaltenden*], a community of those who know their human dignity and hold together as 'human beings.' Our holding together is the *state*; we who hold together are the *nation*."
31. EO, 100
32. EO, 91
33. See EO, 224: "To whoever knows how to take and defend the thing, it belongs, until it is taken away again by another, as freedom belongs to the one who *takes* it."
34. EO, 96–97
35. See Marx, *On the Jewish Question*, MECW 3: 146–175.

We know Stirner read this because he cites it at EO 158, criticizing Marx's use of the concept of "species-being" [*Gattungswesen*]. See note 42.

36. EO, 105
37. *Ibid.*
38. EO, 108
39. Moishe Postone makes a similar criticism of "Traditional Marxism", insofar as it takes labor to be the *standpoint* of critique and not the *object* of the critique of capitalism. See Postone, *Time, Labor, and Social Domination* (1993).
40. EO, 107–8
41. See, for instance, Jean Baudrillard's *The Mirror of Production* (1973), Laclau and Mouffe's *Hegemony and Socialist Strategy* (1985), or, again, Postone (1993).
42. EO, 158: "To identify me now entirely with the human being, the demand has been invented, and stated, that I must become a 'real species being' [*wirkliches Gattungwesen*]." Marx most likely took this concept from Feuerbach, who most likely adapted it from Hegel. Stirner's criticism again emphasizes the *non-identity* of the I.
43. EO, 111
44. EO, 106. *Lump* is translated as "ragamuffin" by Byington and Leopold. "Pauper" or "bum" makes more sense though.
45. EO, 112
46. EO, 118
47. *Ibid.*
48. EO, 159
49. *Ibid.* Stirner never denies that individuals are human, animal, alive, etc. Rather he rejects the claim that such qualities *exhaust* me, or fully identify me. For instance: "You are more than a living essence or animal, this would mean, you are still an animal, but animality does not exhaust what you are." *Stirner's Critics* (2012), 89

Part III: My Stirner

On the rubble of smashed idols, including God, humanity, liberalism, work, the state, and freedom, Stirner begins to lay out his own theory of ownness, the I, and the unique one. But since any positive theory has the potential of becoming a new ruling principle, he repeatedly undoes his project by relating it back to his own nothingness. As owner, I relate to the world through property, power, and ownness; I interact with others and use everything for my own self-enjoyment, as I expect others to do with me. The escape of property from my power into alienty parallels the escape of Stirner's own philosophy from fluidity into dogmas. To Stirner, I should not let my property slip into fixity, just as I should not let myself slip into an identity. "Everything is my own," Stirner declares, "therefore I bring back to myself what wants to escape me; but above all I always bring myself back when I have slipped away from myself into any servitude."[1] This incessant self-persecution, this holding-itself-hostage of the I, exposes the delicate balance between the ego and its own, the unique and its property. But not only that, it also reveals the gap between Stirner and his philosophy, between us and the text as well.

Acknowledging this fragile composition, I will now reconstruct the strange logic of Stirner's argument, step by step. My aim is to give a consistent reading of the text, articulated not in the order Stirner himself laid out, but as I reconstruct it through the text, perhaps even despite it. As Fred Madison said in David Lynch's *Lost Highway*, "I like to remember things my own way. Not necessarily the way they happened." This is one way through the twists and turns of Stirner's argument, *my* way.

I

I am that I am—this is how God introduces himself to Moses, and Stirner follows suit. *I am*—not the tautology of *I am I*, as in Fichte, but a declaration of singularity: I am, this I, me. A seemingly non-controversial starting point, yet we know already that this is not a "presupposition" in the normal sense. It is not the posited fact of being a self that grants validity to starting with the I. Rather, the continuous act of positing myself grants stability to the individuality of I, or at least the appearance of stability. Recall Stirner's disavowal: "I do not presuppose myself, because at any moment I just am positing or creating myself in the first place."[2] This incessant positing and creating is not supported by any *hypokeimenon*, any elemental substrate or immaterial identity; rather, the loop of self-creation is unceasing, occurring only on the surface of nothingness.

In order to make sense of Stirner's unique understanding of the *I*, one should first differentiate it from Fichte's superficially similar use of the same term. A Fichtean interpretation of Stirner would consider the *I* to be a fundamental *a priori* principle—that from which the *particular I* that I am could be deduced. Stirner's "I", however, is always *mine* first, never transcendental. Fichte's "I" is a condition of possibility for experience as such. Stirner's I is not a principle or thesis in the construction of any theoretical system, but a moment in a phenomenological description of experience from the first-person singular perspective.

Although both depart from the *I*, Stirner and Fichte's conceptions are distinct in terms of form and function, content and method. Fichte's transcendental "I", according to Stirner, makes the same error as Feuerbach does with "humanity" and Marx does with "species-being": it imposes an ahistorical and external form on the dynamic content of my existence; it attempts to determine the essence and limits of my experience according to an identity or principle alien to me. It is, in short, an identification of the non-identical. The reasons for this are not just philosophical, but social and political, since each fundamental categorization of the finite I according to some anthropological principle brings along with it social-political consequences for the organization of the state, economy, and society. Stirner wants to stop the machinery of alienation by blocking the initial categorization of the self as something external to its own self-determination. In one of the clearest statements of Stirner's rejection of the unmediated identity of universality and particularity in the coerced fusion of species and I, he writes:

> The species is nothing, and, if the individual lifts himself above the limits of his individuality, this is rather his very self as individual; he exists only in raising himself, he exists only in not remaining what he is; otherwise, he would be done, dead. *The* human being is only an ideal, the species only something thought. To be *a* human is not to realize the ideal of *the human being*, but to present *oneself*, the individual. It is not how I realize the universal human that needs to be my task, but how I satisfy myself. *I* am my species, am without norm, without law, without model, etc. It is possible that I can make very little out of myself; but this little is everything, and is better than what I allow to be made out of me by the might of others, by the training of custom, religion, the laws, the state.[3]

Without norm, without law, without model—*I* am nothing but what I make of myself, *against* my constraints, even if this turns out to be very little indeed. Stirner's radical break with *a priorism* and all kinds of determinism—biological, metaphysical, material—strongly suggests an absolute freedom of the contingent I to determine its own conditions of possibility. Fichte's transcendental I, and other similar forms of self-identification, must therefore be rejected.[4]

A different, more adequate interpretation of Stirner's I is that it begins where Hegel's *Phenomenology of Spirit* ends.[5] The dialectic of spirit ends in absolute knowledge, the moment when I truly know myself as I, *this I* which experiences itself as the movement and result of self-consciousness. As the mediated unity of subjective and objective consciousness, the self-aware, self-differentiating subject of absolute knowing does not rest in its "final" status. Rather, satisfied with the relation between its universal form and particular content, the I can finally *begin* to consume everything as its own.[6] In the final chapter of the *Phenomenology of Spirit* on "Absolute Knowing", Hegel makes this clear:

> The nature, moments and movement of this [absolute] knowing have thus turned out to be such that this knowing is the pure *being-for-itself* of self-consciousness; it is 'I', which is *this I* and no other, and is just as much the immediately *mediated* or sublated [*aufgehobenes*] *universal* 'I'. — It has a *content* that it *differentiates* from itself, for it is pure negativity or the dividing of itself; it is *consciousness*. This content is, in its differences, itself the 'I', for it is the movement of sublating itself, or the same pure negativity that is the 'I'.[7]

Usually glossed over in Hegel's concept of absolute knowing is its radical negativity, its power as a force of dissolution of everything separate from the I, everything alien to it. Stirner's *I* begins from this radically negative standpoint of absolute knowledge, which now has no need to reflect backwards on its dialectical progression. On the contrary, the task is to move radically forward, consuming every obstacle in its path. This *negativity* of the I — its restless labor of dissolving externality into itself — propels Stirner's negations of all fixed ideas. As Lawrence Stepelevich correctly notes,

> His particular complementing of Hegel consisted in taking the 'we' of Hegel's *Phenomenology* — that constant observer and sometimes director of the course of knowledge from its beginning in apparent sense-certainty to its conclusion

in absolute knowledge—as *himself*... Stirner, however, does not give himself either the name 'I' or 'Stirner' but rather introduces into philosophical literature a new term intended to convey the note of radical exclusiveness, a term that would lie outside of all classifications: '*Der Einzige.*'[8]

Whereas Hegel's task is to raise thought to the level of spirit, Stirner's goal is to bring spirit back down to *me*. Only *I*, he says, as the unique one [*Einzige*] can do this. Stirner asks,

> Who, then, will dissolve the spirit into its *nothing*? He who by means of spirit presented nature as *nothing*, finite, transitory, he alone can bring down spirit too to the same nothingness. *I* can do it, each one of you can who rules and creates as an unlimited I; in a word—the *egoist* can.[9]

The I that can do this does not emerge merely out of the path of negation, but also in an act of radical affirmation: *I can*. Stirner thus not only presupposes Hegel's science of the experience of consciousness, he *consumes* it.

Individuals

Stirner begins by affirming the unique individuality of the *I* against all attempts to classify it, limit it. But how is this I an *individual*? It is not so easy to decipher the meaning of individuality in Stirner. To say that the *I* is an individual seems obvious, and yet, to determine the limits of individuality poses all sorts of metaphysical conundrums. The problem is not about what constitutes the essence of an individual, that is, some ideal unity, material cohesion, reason, name, etc. That question either ignores or takes for granted *who* this individual already is. The issue is rather about the *scale* and *meaning* of individuality as an ontological category.

Stirner's dangerous question according to Deleuze, the

question which unraveled and ruined the dialectic, is *Which one*?[10] Which one is the subject of absolute knowing, which I bears the spirit of history? We can ask the same question concerning the individual: Which individual? Which individuality? A common assumption is that the individuality of the I is guaranteed by its body. The body is *one*, and since the self-positing, self-dissolving current of the I is empirically indistinguishable from the solid unity of the body, we can safely assume that the I is *one* as well. If individuality is established with reference to corporeally distinct human beings, then affirming the sovereignty of the I entails privileging human beings as individual *persons*. An individual, therefore, is a person.

Stirner rejects this. His argument is not anthropological, in fact cares little for anthropology, man, or the human species. He derides the political viewpoint that privileges human beings above all as "anthropocracy," the rule of man.[11] The point is rather ontological. The individuals that Stirner describes are entities, individuated bodies that reject formalization. We can see this most clearly in his persistent attack on generalities, which he calls spooks or specters. A generality is always deceptive to Stirner, perhaps necessary, but deceptive nonetheless. To unquestionably believe in generalities is to theologize, to import essences behind things, to act like the adolescent "Christian" who trusts in spirits, the citizen who believes in the state or the bourgeois who has faith in the market. Although this may seem like a kind of nominalism, it is not. For Stirner does not deny the existence of universals, he only denies their absoluteness, their unconditionality. To Stirner, universals are *one-sided*, incomplete expressions of truth. They thus must be domesticated, qualified and mediated through the singularity of individuals.

Stirner makes this clear when he criticizes humane liberalism for trying to fix a ground for equality between individuals in some common identity or trait: "I do not count myself as anything special, but as *unique*. Without a doubt, I am similar to others;

however, this holds good only for comparison or reflection; in fact, I am incomparable, unique. My flesh is not their flesh, my mind is not their mind. If you bring them under the generalities 'flesh, mind', those are your *thoughts,* which have nothing to do with *my* flesh, *my* mind."[12] Stirner does not disclaim the existence of general comparisons between individuals, but mediates them as partial representations of singularities. Even my flesh and mind—metonyms for the material and immaterial sides of my I—are also individual, uniquely incomparable parts of myself. Parts of myself, that is, qualities, characteristics, and properties, can also be conceived as *individual.* Their generality is only warranted by an epistemological or linguistic necessity. Deepening this reflection on the problem of universals, Stirner writes,

> We are equal *only in thoughts,* only when 'we' are *thought,* not as we really and bodily are. I am I, and you are I: but I am not this thought-of I; this I in which we are all equal is only *my thought.* I am human, you are human: but 'human' is only a thought, a generality; neither you and I are speakable, we are *unutterable,* because only *thoughts* are speakable and consist in speaking.[13]

The generic equality between you and I as "we" does exist— *in thought.* Thoughts, universals, generalities are not unreal, but they are not all reality. The singularity of the individual can never be fully expressed in thought or speech, for both are partial expressions of the infinite negativity of I. To Stirner, speech is not a screen of transparent communication from one individual to the next, but a generalization of one's individuality thrown against the generalization of another. The individual does not coincide with the speaking subject, but rather defies it. In this sense, individuality can only be *thought* as the movement of resistance within and against the logic of generalization.

Otherwise, it is not thought at all, but enacted.

In another example, Stirner claims that the shift from Christian identity to the "newly discovered" human identity is only a step forward *within* religion, not *out of* religion.[14] For "the subject is again subjected to the predicate, the individual to something general."[15] The political form of humanism is the state, that structure which "has the sole purpose to limit, tame, subordinate, the individual—to make him subject to some *generality* or other."[16] The individual is therefore the "irreconcilable enemy of every *generality*."[17] However, subjection and predication occur not only with individual persons, but with *any* individual case of which we can speak and think. The individual subjected to a predicate, "tamed" by a generality, can be this paper, that shadow, his smile, her kiss. Any of these things can be generalized away from the singularity of their existence into something other. In this sense, individuality does not entail the specific negation of generality, but rather a condition of it.

For Kant, the structuring of the manifold of experiences and objects is subsumed under the general categories of reason, and made coherent through the transcendental unity of apperception. For Stirner, reason's labor of subsumption violates the singularity of individuals. This is why individuals, in the end, cannot be fully comprehended. To Stirner, "only thoughtlessness really saves me from thoughts. It is not thinking, but my thoughtlessness, or I the unthinkable, incomprehensible, that frees me from possession."[18]

Possession here signifies being possessed by dogmas of thought. But individuals possessed by ideological spirits cannot exorcise themselves through thinking alone, since thoughts can never every fully escape their universal form of presentation. And this form itself is the problem for Stirner, for reason and language necessarily mutate every singularity into a universal. To break this sequence is to strike against the immanent production of transcendental illusions, a seemingly impossible task.

In this schema, not only are subjects considered individuals, but objects too. Yet, if everything that exists is ultimately an individual, then what is the status of universals? The problem of universals was a key issue in medieval and early modern philosophy, and still resonates in contemporary metaphysics.[19] To Hobbes, "universals" do not exist *except* as common names used to describe the diversity of singular things: "There being nothing in the world universal but names; for the things named are every one of them individual and singular."[20] The convention of universal names is necessary, according to this view, because grasping the individuality of every object is impossible for the human mind. It would overload the ability to think across differences, crushing the capacity for generalization.

Locke already criticized this in his *Essay Concerning Human Understanding*: "It is impossible that every particular thing should have a distinct peculiar name... It is beyond the power of human capacity to frame and retain distinct *ideas* of all particular things we meet with: every bird, and beast men saw; every tree, and plant, that affected the senses, could not find a place in the most capacious understanding."[21] Jorge Luis Borges brilliantly fictionalized this quandary in his short story, *Funes the Memorious*. The protagonist, Funes, remembers every particular thing, and thus does not grasp universals. This makes it impossible for Funes to truly *think*. Since, as Borges writes at the end of the story, "To think is to forget differences, to generalize, to abstract. In the crowded world of Funes, there were only details—almost immediate."[22]

Stirner does not advocate this super-nominalism, as Leibniz once called the philosophy of Hobbes.[23] He recognizes the problem, and seeks another strategy: to stop trying to *think* one's way out of universals altogether. One cannot simply think or speak their way out of generalization, and thus, out of ideology. The solution can only be *practical*, as a particular orientation towards everything external to oneself. Such a practice will eventually be called *consumption* by Stirner. I will come back to this later.

Stirner's text does not decide on what can and cannot be an individual. However, my aim is to extrapolate a consistent reading of Stirner's argument, and the only way to do this is to take Stirner's *individuals* as global phenomena, not limited to "human egos." If this is wrong, then the rest of the text falls into the anthropocentrism that it so clearly derides. Furthermore, this interpretation opens up a pathway between the dead-ends of a debilitating overthinking and a mindless nonthought. To follow through on this reading, one would have to construct an ontology that extends the existence of singular individuals to all things; this is exactly what Spinoza does in his *Ethics*.

It is my contention that Stirner's individualism should be read in the same way we read Spinoza's individualism. It is an ontological statement about *what there is*, not a moral statement about individual persons. Stirner's only fault lies in stopping his critique at the level of epistemology. In any case, it is possible to reconstruct an ontology that makes sense of Stirner's views. Spinoza's philosophical system describes just this.

Spinoza

What do we experience in Spinoza's universe? Only *singular things*. How is that possible? In nature, there is "only one substance" and this substance is infinite in its attributes, modes, and essence.[24] Every particular thing in the world must somehow be an *immanent expression* of this essence. There is nothing outside this substance and "there is no vacuum in nature."[25] But if there is no outside, then how can we still have a coherent idea of *expression*? For to express something, like an essence, there usually has to be an external or transcendent body, field, or plane to which or in which the expressing activity is directed. Any activity occurring in a closed system is contained absolutely *within* that system. Thus, expression in one substance would be a contradiction of terms.

To express an essence, however, is not to *exhibit* something in a directional or vectorial manner, but rather to *manifest* a certain logic in the internal organization of that object. A better word would be *composition*, not expression. For the idea of composition need not assume an outside, nor barely even an inside. All composition assumes is a pure relation between elements or variables which, when organized in a certain manner, retain a unique identity. To retain a unique identity is the defining property of a *singularity*. What is a singularity? In Book II of the *Ethics*, Spinoza makes the following definition: "By singular thing, I understand things that are finite and have a determinate existence. And if a number of individuals so concur in one action that together they are all the cause of one effect, I consider them all, to that extent, as one singular thing."[26] There are two main points here which should be dealt with separately.

First, singular things are finite, determinate individuals, which are, in Spinoza's framework, finite manifestations or effects of an infinitely determined causal series. A body, a thought, an object, or anything meeting these two conditions qualifies as a singular thing. We experience the smell of a flower, the touch of another human being, the taste of an apple, the sound of a voice. In each case, we experience singular entities under different attributes. But these examples are too simple, for we assume that the singularity of an object is identical to its appearance as an individual body under different sensory impressions. Here, Spinoza's definition can be of great help: the singularity of a thing is not just the transposition of its singular extended body into an individual identity, rather a singular thing can be any number of individual bodies which, *in one action*, collectively cause a single effect. At first this seems blurred. Are we not conflating causal motion with individual identity? In fact, that is exactly what we are doing, and it is nevertheless an incredibly liberating conceptual move.

By binding the meaning of "singular" to the meaning of "action" and "effect", Spinoza allows plurality to be equally as significant as individuality in the determination of a singular thing. Decoupling the meaning of singular from the meaning of individual shatters the conception of identity as a property of an individual. An individual does not have an identity except in its relation to a series of causes and effects which are determined by other individuals, which themselves have no identity except in their relation to a series of causes and effects, and so on *ad infinitum*. The identity of an individual is not then based on an internal property, but on an external relation of *action* and *effect*. How can many things be one individual, and how can many individuals be one singular thing? Through their *composition* in forming a single effect, whether or not their individual causes are completely different.

Owners

Now that we have an account which can make sense of Stirner's radical individualism without lapsing into a naive psychologism or an anthropocentric egoism, we can push forward. This interlude on Spinoza will have proven to be worthwhile in grasping the steps to come.

If individuality is a properly ontological category, then what distinguishing mark interrupts the homogeneity of individual beings so that we can recognize their differences? In other words, what is the individual's status vis-à-vis other individuals? What separates individuals from blending into each other? From the point of view of ontology, nothing differentiates individuals except their concurrence into one causally effective action or another. But from the point of view of the individual, however, the situation is different.

For Stirner, individuals are distinct in their capacity to be owners [*Eigner*]. To be an owner is to be more than a bare individual; it is to recognize one's individuality, to be self-consciously, explicitly singular. In Hegelian terms, such an individual is not merely *in-itself*, but *for-itself*. An owner is one who marks out the singularity of their existence by *owning* their properties, and not being enslaved to them. The category "property" casts a net as wide as the term "object", in fact wider, for it also means qualities, characteristics, and styles. An owner is one who determines their own relation to an object such that they, in the end, can annul it. If one's property is incapable of being annulled, then it is not property *per se*, but fixity, alienated property, *alienty*.

Owners, in other words, *make themselves* individuals. An owner is not formed through a higher calling or a given cause. To be an owner is to individuate oneself through the appropriation of one's own conditions and the dissolution of everything alien to them. One who submits to another's property forfeits their ownership in that regard, and concedes their power. With Spinoza, we could say that the owner's ability to make something its property, its individuality, is its ability to cause and determine a certain effect. If an owner cannot appropriate through its action, then its individuality is in question.

Since there are always generalities, spooks, and fixed ideas floating around in our heads (for we all deal in language and thoughts), there is only one way to ensure complete ownership and complete individuality. We must own *ourselves*. If we are able to determine our entire being such that we are willing and have the power to dissolve it as a whole, then we have made ourselves into property; we have made ourselves singular individuals. Whatever relations we have with property, owned or subjugated, we at least own ourselves, such that our being is secure. If we do not own ourselves, then whatever desire, style, or end—that is, whatever property—we may control, there will *always* be an excess, out-of-control, beyond it. Losing property and losing oneself does not only occur when one is careless about oneself, but also when one is *too* caring for oneself. Selfishness is just as much a false idol as unselfishness, for both attitudes determine our activity separate from our own individual development. They are forms without content:

> A purpose ceases to be *our* purpose and our *property*, which we, as owners, can dispose of at pleasure; where it becomes a fixed purpose or a—fixed idea; where it begins to inspire, enthuse, fanaticize us; in short, where it passes into our *dogmatism* and becomes our—master.[27]

As finite, limited individuals, we cannot account for all, and hence we must account for ourselves to make up for that lack. But *how* we account for ourselves is just as important as why.

Property

The individual as such is indiscernible. Only in one's role as an *owner* does individuality manifest itself for-itself. Being an owner means having a certain relationship to property such that one has the final say in how that property holds.

But if owners are only defined by their relation to property, and if all relations to property by the owner are fundamentally the same, then we still have not really individuated one owner from the next. We have elicited the owner *from oneself*, and can distinguish whether one is an owner or not, but we have not determined how distinct owners differ. If the ability to be an owner is structurally the same for all individuals, then the difference between owners can only emerge on the side of their property. In other words, it is not just the *ability* to produce a single effect that individuates an owner, but the history of such effects that one has caused as well. Therefore, *what* the owners own is as significant as how one owns it.

One of Stirner's most frequent targets—besides God, the church, truth, the state, and liberalism—is *humanity*, or man.

The idea of the "human being" is not significant in itself; it only affects an individual if one makes it into one of their *properties*. In that sense, it becomes one of the innumerable qualities which sets the owner apart. To *only* notice one's humanity is just as one-sided as only noticing one's gender. For Stirner, "That we are human is the least thing about us, and only has significance in so far as it is one of our *qualities* [*Eigenschaften*], that is, our property [*Eigentum*]. I am indeed among other things a human being, as I am a living being, therefore an animal, or a European, a Berliner, and the like; but he who chose to regard me only as a human being, or as a Berliner, would pay me little regard indeed. And why? Because he would only have noticed one of my *qualities*, not *me*."[28] To be more or *less* than human is one's own prerogative. An owner, then, is dependent on its properties for its singular differentiation, not only for its singular identification. The collection of unique properties, or the series of unique effects, marks the history of an individual as an owner apart from others.

"What then is *my* property?" Stirner asks. "Nothing but what is in my *power!* To which property am I entitled? To everything which I—*empower myself*. I give myself the right to property in taking property for myself, or giving myself the property owner's *power*, full power, empowerment."[29] Property does not itself name the object which I own, but rather the relation of *power* between the object and myself mediated by others. Property is *mine* insofar as the power to appropriate it—or better put, *expropriate* it—is mine. For property only becomes one's own through taking. Whether the object expropriated is a material thing or spiritual idea, anything can become my property. I have the power to make it so, and power, as a relation, is ontologically indiscriminate. "Let me claim as property everything that I feel myself strong enough to attain," Stirner announces, "and let me extend my actual property as far as *I* entitle, that is, empower, myself to take."[30]

To own property is thus not a right to Stirner, but an act of self-empowerment. Property is always *self*-empowering because the power to expropriate is in *me*, not something granted by others. Neither law nor family nor religion grants rights to property. What backs up the claim to ownership is the power to defend what's mine, alone or with others.

"Everything over which I have power that cannot be torn from me remains my property."[31] But my power can be yours as well when we join together to expropriate the property of another. By expropriating external things and making them mine, I expand my capacities for action, and thus expand my self. I gain no legal right to exclude others from my use of things. All I acquire is the objective confirmation of my capacity to act in the world, to have an effect on my surroundings, to consume, dissolve, and negate the solidity of my given conditions, and put them to new uses. I acquire, in short, control over my own alienation.

Stirner's materialist view of property as a relation of power is much closer to the realist theories of Machiavelli, Hobbes, and Rousseau then it is to the rights-based theories of Locke, Kant or Hegel. Yet, whereas all the above political philosophers seek to tame the violence of property through a coercive state apparatus with authority, Stirner recognizes that such an authority only displaces the power of expropriation to a more abstract, alienated level. Thus, he urges individuals to take for themselves whatever they can, to empower themselves through the expropriation of property instead of limiting themselves through the renunciation of power.

Stirner's concept of power, however, remains ambiguous. I have power, I take power, I am power—in acknowledging my power over myself, I own myself. In owning myself, I become my own property, capable of being disposed, and thus powerless. "My power is *my* property. My power *gives* me property. My power *am* I myself, and through it am I my property."[32] I am all and nothing—creator and created, owner and owned, possessor and possessed, split between my power to determine myself and my capacity to be determined. There is no simple unity that transcends this division of the I; it is reproduced through the continual process of expropriating and being expropriated. The task of Stirner's *unique one* is to own and develop the means of expropriation, and thus, the means of individuation. This does not take place by means of rights but through my power: "Right—is a wheel in the head, put there by a spook; power—that am I myself, I am the powerful one and owner of power."[33] To sacrifice power for right is to voluntarily submit to rule by alienation. The point, however, is to make right into one's property, and consume it.

Nietzsche

Nietzsche has a theory of power as strange and central as Stirner's. The cryptic idea of the *will to power* names the elemental force chaotically weaving together Nietzsche's universe. Above all, this is the power to interpret, to act, create, and become something *individual*, unique. The proximity of thought between Stirner and Nietzsche has been a topic of debate since the 1890s. Eduard von Hartmann—who Nietzsche read and criticized in his *On the Use and Abuse of History for Life*—publicly accused Nietzsche of plagiarizing Stirner (as Marx accused Stirner of plagiarizing Hegel).[34] The answer to that question is still up in the air.[35]

Nietzsche's early essay on *History* is significant here for a number of reasons. First, the title itself mimics Stirner's understanding of what defines property, namely, *use and abuse*. Nietzsche's analysis is a story of the consumption of history as property, its use and abuse by different owners. Second, Nietzsche's criticisms of Hartmann's book, *Philosophy of the Unconscious*, deal exactly with those sections where Hartmann mentions and criticizes Stirner. In contrast to Hartmann, Nietzsche advises that each person should seek out the *individual that they are*, and not relegate oneself to a herd-mentality. More than that, the individual should create their own goals and meaning. Nietzsche writes,

> But do ask what you, the individual, are there for, and if no one else can tell you then just try sometime to justify the meaning of your existence *a posteriori*, as it were, by setting yourself a purpose, a goal, a 'for this', a lofty and noble 'for this.' And perish in the attempt—I know of no better life's purpose than to perish, *animae magnae prodigus*, in attempting the great and impossible.[36]

In one of Stirner's similar moments of ethical clarity, he describes how one should use up life "like the candle, which one uses in burning up."[37] Later in the same essay, Nietzsche praises the Greeks for *owning themselves*, for "taking possession" of themselves, controlling their needs, their properties. Nietzsche:

> The Greeks learned gradually *to organize chaos* by reflecting on themselves in accordance with the Delphic teaching, that is, by reflecting on their genuine needs, and letting their sham needs die out. Thus they took possession of themselves again... This is a parable for each one of us: he must organize the chaos within himself by reflecting on his genuine needs.[38]

Nietzsche's thinking on individuality, power, and self-possession did not end there. In his final notebooks, spuriously gathered together as one single work under the title *The Will to Power*, the question of the individual occupies him even more.[39]

For Stirner, every individual as an owner is also the result of the series of properties it has consumed. For Nietzsche, "every individual consists of the whole course of evolution."[40] If we allow a wide interpretation of *consumption* and *property*, then Stirner's statement is already evolutionary. To Nietzsche,

The individual is something quite new which creates new things, something absolute; all his acts are entirely his own. Ultimately, the individual derives the values of his acts from himself; because he has to interpret in a quite individual way even the words he has inherited. His interpretation of a formula at least is personal, even if he does not create a formula: as an interpreter he is still creative.[41]

The individual contains the history of its evolution. Nonetheless, it is *unique*. It interprets, that is, consumes and owns its world as well as its values. "All its acts are entirely its own." Even expropriating something of another can still be a "creative" act. Nietzsche:

The 'I' subdues and kills: it operates like an organic cell: it is a robber and violent. It wants to regenerate itself—pregnancy. It wants to give birth to its god and see all mankind at his feet.[42]

Nietzsche's description of the individual I parallels Stirner's portrayal of the all-consuming and all-dissolving individual owner, the I that expropriates and destroys its property in order to remain unique. The I acquires its content through the theft of experience; it is a "criminal" in Stirner's vocabulary, set against every attempt to capture it. Continually regenerating itself, presupposing itself, consuming itself—the I never rests. While Nietzsche's individual gives birth to gods, Stirner's I *consumes* them. This is perhaps the greatest difference between Stirner and Nietzsche. Stirner eats gods, dissolving their potency and using their power for himself. Nietzsche births gods, creating new ones beyond himself that one day will exceed him as well.[43]

For Nietzsche, as with Stirner, there is nothing hidden beneath the mask of the ego; the "ego" as such is an illusion, a spook projected onto those who do not conform to the image of a proper subject, citizen, worker, consumer, or human being. "The 'subject' is only a fiction," Nietzsche writes, "the ego of which one speaks when one censures egoism does not exist at all."[44] This does not mean that individuals do not exist, only that there is no generic individual. Each I is constituted by the singular history of its actions and conditions, property and consumption.

Stirner and Nietzsche both mock the socialism of their day, but their targets and reasons are different. Stirner's derision towards "social liberalism" and what he calls "communism" is a critique of utopian socialist ideology of the 1840s, not a denunciation of actual workers' struggles or revolts of the poor and oppressed. For Nietzsche, the actual socialist movements are nothing more than expressions of slave morality, decrepit egalitarianism, and bad health. Also, their "collectivism" betrays a weak kind of individualism, one which reflects a modest, unconscious stage of the will to power:

> *Individualism* is a modest and unconscious form of the 'will to power'; here it seems sufficient to the individual to get free from an overpowering domination by society (whether that of the state or of the church). He does not oppose them as a person, but only as an individual; he represents all individuals against the totality... Socialism is merely a means of agitation employed by individualism: it grasps that, to attain anything, one must organize to a collective action, to a 'power'... Anarchism, too, is merely a means of agitation employed by socialism; by means of it, socialism arouses fear, by means of fear it begins to fascinate and to terrorize: above all—it draws the courageous, the daring to its side, even in the most spiritual matters. All this notwithstanding: individualism is the *most modest* stage of the will to power.[45]

Nietzsche reads Stirner's individualism as the secret motivation behind socialism, since socialism only ever desires a collectivist order of equal egos. This weak individualism does not rise to the true overcoming that Nietzsche seeks. Whereas Nietzsche understands the individual as only one expression of the will to power, Stirner's *Einzige* does not express any other deeper force, for any other constraint would bind the radical singularity of the I to another property, and hence, rob it of its unconditioned nature. One could interpret Nietzsche's criticism of weak individualism similarly to Stirner's critique of humane liberalism. In that case, the stated individualism is only individualism-for-another-purpose, e.g., humanity, the good, etc. Stirner's immodest egoism cares little for such causes. Nietzsche, however, still remains enthralled by a spook, a cause beyond himself—the will to power. Stirner ultimately lets go of that as well.

Expropriation

How does the owner relate to its property? Proudhon, in his 1840 treatise *What is Property?*, writes: "Roman law defined property as the right to use and abuse one's own within the limits of the law—*jus utendi et abutendi re sua, quatenus iuris ratio patitur.*"[46] He then illustrates the continued use of this definition in the Declaration of Rights of Man of 1793 and in the Napoleonic Code of 1804, article 544. Distinguishing between property and possession, he states that the former concerns absolute domain and sovereignty over the thing (*naked property*), whereas the latter concerns only a "matter of fact." To clarify this distinction, he offers a comparison: if "a lover is a possessor," then "a husband is a proprietor."[47] Proudhon's aim is to defend possession against property, to prove the injustice behind the so-called "natural right" of property, and argue for its abolition.

"What is property?" Proudhon wonders. *Property is theft!* A robbery of our common nature and our common labor. *Possession*, on the other hand, is a necessary part of social life; it is the temporary use of things for personal purposes. Possession cannot be abolished, since it is intrinsic to all human societies, a fact of life. Stirner clearly lifts his definition of property from Proudhon, but instead of advocating for its abolition, he radicalizes it. Stirner asserts,

> Property is the expression for *unlimited dominion* over something (thing, animal, human being) which 'I can dispose of at my will.' According to Roman law, indeed, *'ius utendi et abutendi re sua, quatenus iuris ratio patitur'*, an *exclusive* and *unlimited right*; but property is conditioned by power. What I have in my power, that is my own. As long as I assert myself as possessor, I am the owner of the thing; if it gets away from me again, no matter by what power, for instance, through my recognition of another's claim to the thing—then the property is lost. Thus, property and possession coincide. No right lying outside my power legitimizes me, but solely my power: if I no longer have it, then the thing slips away from me.[48]

Instead of seeing property as a relation constrained by law, Stirner takes property solely as a relation of power *against the law*. The law, as fixed idea and norm, constrains my power, blocks it and gives my property to the state; the law determines what I can and cannot own, and since law is the property of the state, the state is the ultimate owner of my property. To be an owner in Stirner's sense of the term, that is, an owner *against* the law and state, does not mean that one should renounce private property in favor of small-scale personal possession. Stirner does not see the benefit in abolishing private property and returning it to the so-called original possessor of "society" or some "board of equity", as Proudhon proclaims. That would only transfer the power to expropriate to someone else, and thus, grant others the right to steal from me. The goal is rather to empty the idea of property of *any sacred right whatsoever*, to desecrate it, loot its content.

To call property theft is to presuppose the concept of property and to criticize theft, whereas for Stirner, property should be praised since it first allows the possibility of theft! "Property is not theft, but a theft becomes possible only through property."[49]

Theft is not intrinsically *wrong*, to Stirner. Rather, he thinks that theft is just one way of changing ownership. If he believed in rights, which he does not, then he would say that everyone has a right to steal. For Stirner, property has nothing to do with protecting or securing my liberty; it rather forms the basis for mutual violation—a *positive* social relation. When no one can violate the property of another, when no one can take another's property for themselves, then all remain powerless. Since the true basis of property according to Proudhon lies in labor and society, he proposes to safeguard personal possessions and abolish property. Stirner conversely suggests associating in common for the sake of taking the property of the few:

> There are some things that belong only to a few, and to which the rest of us will now lay claim or—siege. Let us take them, because one comes to property by taking, and the property we still lack now came to the owners also only by taking. It can be better put to use if it is in *all our hands* than if the few control it. Let us therefore associate ourselves for the purpose of this robbery (*vol*).[50]

Yet, Proudhon remains enamored by ghosts. Instead of recognizing the contingency and force at the source of property relations, he considers the "spook of society as a *moral person*,"[51] as the original possessor and sole proprietor, as that spirit to whom we should return the stolen goods. Although Proudhon calls himself an anarchist, he makes the same error as the liberals, Christians and communists. In one way or another, according to Stirner, all of them replace the individual and its power with some alien cause and its authority.[52] For Stirner, there is only one law of property: "Whoever knows how to take and to claim the thing, to them it belongs until it is again taken from them, as freedom belongs to those who *take* it."[53]

All property follows the logic of occupation. To own is to occupy, to deploy force in relation to things and persons; property names this activity, not the thing. "My property is not a thing, since this has an existence independent of me; only my power is my own. Not this tree, but my power or disposal over it, is what is mine."[54]

Stirner thus interprets property as a form of squatting, and justifies it. If property is a relation of power between individuals concerning external things, then the limits of property extend to the limits of one's power to claim and defend something as their own. This understanding of property suggests the same strategy that Marx and Kropotkin all thought were essential if the poorest class was ever to succeed in regaining its power and dignity: *expropriation*. To expropriate in this sense does not mean to turn over private property to the state for the public good, but to take the property of another for one's own good, one's own friends or class, as it were. Whether accomplished by oneself or united with others, whether against capitalists, bureaucrats, or the state, expropriation is the self-emancipation of the *Einzige*.

Everyone is either an expropriator or an expropriated. Property must therefore be taken in order to be owned, not petitioned, protested or bought. Stirner's point is that expropriation is not just a means of responding to the contemporary distribution of wealth; rather, *expropriation is internal to the logic of property as such*. All property is based on expropriation in some sense. This does not invalidate it, but reveals its truth. No one is going to simply give up their "unjustly" acquired property to a public authority. Everyone must take the chance to expropriate for themselves. Stirner calls this *self-empowerment*. Anything less is charity.

Consumption

Property names a relation of power, a certain manifestation of force that binds an object to an owner without it in turn determining the owner itself. Since property is not guaranteed by any authority to Stirner, it is ultimately precarious, continuously at risk of being lost. Property can be lost in two ways: it can either be taken by another (through someone else's power)[55] or it can transform into something else—fixed, solid, and sacred. If I do not keep guard over myself and my property, what I consider *mine* can become *other*, it can become my owner. This is the process of alienation and reification outlined earlier in relation to *fixed ideas*.

It is easier to protect one's property from someone else than it is to guard it from oneself. To own something is a practice, a technique or skill that must be continually renewed in relation to the object at hand; if not, the property relation will harden, coagulate, and petrify. In order to secure one's property against this particular kind of threat, one must constantly destroy its separation from the owner. That is, one must consume it, dissolve and annihilate it. The loss of property is the triumph of its autonomization. Any relation that escapes the power of individuals to control it is doomed. Stirner: "I want only to take care that I secure my property to myself; and, in order to secure it, I continually take it back into myself, annihilate it in every movement toward independence and consume it before it can fix itself and become a 'fixed idea' or an 'addiction'."[56] If property becomes an addiction or obsession, then it controls me, determines me; it is not mine, but I am its. The addict's relation to its own property is a *fixation*, as Freud might say, a pathological investment of power in an object or relation that fixes the ego in a particular stage of development; fixed ideas and addictions to particular properties are thus symptoms of a blocked *besetzung*.[57] When this occurs, I am no longer my *own*. I am *occupied* [*besetzt*] or *possessed* [*besessen*] by the thing.

To maintain myself *against* my property, I must then devour it whole.

To know whether *I own property* or *property owns me* is then the test of its abuse, violation, and destruction. To destroy property is to reveal who is the true owner of it. When workers go on strike and destroy their own tools, when youth riot, burn their own neighborhoods and loot their own stores, when students occupy their own universities and render them inoperative, it is an assertion of ownership over the property in question, an assertion of power that validates the criteria of who and what rules. If a thing cannot be nothing to me, then it is not properly mine.[58]

Consumption, for Stirner, describes the real process by which an owner abolishes the separated power of the object of property. The form of consumption extends to all possible kinds of interaction between the ego and its own: eating, criticizing, wasting, wearing, whatever. To consume is to temporarily dissolve the gap between the subjective and objective sides of experience, to erase the independence and power of the owned, and compound the independence and power of the owner. To Stirner, consumption is the means by which fixed ideas, relations, and objects lose their external and objective form, and are released into free use.

To be clear, consumption does not mean the abolition of mediation in general or the celebration of pure immediacy; those are the delusional fantasies of a childlike ego. Rather, consumption *incorporates* its mediations, absorbs them into one's power as property to be used and abused at will. There is no I without relationality, separation, or mediation; those are parts of oneself as much as anything else. To consume them is to dissolve their *power* over me, their capacity to determine me against myself. Domination can appear in myriad guises— immediately and mediated, directly and indirectly. One should thus beware of welcoming the content of slavery in the form of freedom. Indeed, binding one's liberation to a fixed and frozen form of experience ensures the loss of oneself into a petrified state of being.

Out of consumption, I create myself. This unique pool of nothing into and out of which property flows is only conceivable when ripped from its activity and stabilized in thought and words. This analytic procedure punctures the flow of consuming, dissolving and creating, and allows for the owner to be named: *I*. But as Stirner repeats, this is only a thought-of I, not a living I. I cannot be fixed in language any more than I can fix language once and for all. This problem should not be avoided or mystified, but consumed. That means, recognizing the power of language over me, and letting go of trying to conquer it from within. Stirner writes,

> I have thoughts only as *human*; as I, I am at the same time *thoughtless*. One who cannot get rid of a thought is so far *only* human, is a slave to *language*, this human institution, this treasury of *human* thoughts. Language or 'the word' tyrannizes hardest over us, because it brings up against us a whole army of *fixed ideas*. Just observe yourself in the act of reflection, right now, and you will find how you make progress only by becoming thoughtless and speechless every moment. You are not thoughtless and speechless merely in (say) sleep, but even in the deepest reflection; yes, precisely then most so. And only by this thoughtlessness, this unrecognized 'freedom of thought' or freedom from thought, are you your own. Only from this do you succeed in consuming language as your *property*.[59]

Thinking and speaking are fundamental properties of the human being. Fine, Stirner retorts, but I do not want to be just *human*. To be merely human is to adapt oneself to a generic category, an empty container in which the dead weight of stale tradition and social convention predetermines the limits of one's thoughts and the meaning of one's words. Stirner rather wants to eat language and chew on history, to masticate and spit out half-baked concepts, to consume and be consumed by others in his own peculiar way. To step off the rails of thinking involves withdrawing from common patterns of thought, dissolving their autonomous power, and letting the unthought come to the fore. Whether this involves releasing the unconscious, confronting the uncanny, or speaking the taboo, Stirner is open to the infinite possibilities that arise when one stops trying to force oneself into processed containers of meaning.

Consuming language, or putting it to use as one's property, means freely creating, negating, and developing words and thoughts at will. To balance thinking with thoughtlessness, at Stirner recommends, means circumventing the confines of petrified concepts, freeing oneself from the traditions of past categories, classifications, and identities. Thoughtlessness is not some mystical disengagement from life. On the contrary, it is an acute attentiveness to oneself and to the unconscious presuppositions of one's thinking and speaking. For only through disciplined focus can one avoid becoming ensnared in one's own head. To abstain from the temptation of certain general ideas takes work, perhaps training. In another era, Stirner might have even been called a *Stoic*.

Ownness

The owner differentiates itself from other individuals through its property. However, as an owner, I am not *exhausted* by my property, since I can still consume it in full, dissolving everything I own. Because the owner can act upon *all* its property and yet still maintain itself separate from its property, it necessarily *exceeds* its property. This excess or surplus of the owner against its property only appears in the process of consumption, in the proof that one is separate from one's properties. For in consumption the owner negates the property that distinguishes itself from others as unique. If I was only my property, Stirner might say, then I too would be lost in consumption. But I am not; I am non-identical with my property, always more, or less than it. This surplus of being can also be seen as a *lack* from another point of view. To be more than one's property means that something is missing in relation to it, something left unexpressed, unrepresented. Stirner's *Einzige* is never fully present in its property since it resists determination in any single form. Stirner calls this non-identity of the unique and its property—*ownness* [*Eigenheit*]:

> Ownness is my whole being and existence, it is I myself. I am free from what I am *rid* of, owner of what I have in my *power* or of which I am *powerful*. I am at all times and under all circumstances *my own*, if I know how to have myself and do not throw myself away on others. To be free is something that I cannot truly *will*, because I cannot make it, cannot create it: I can only wish it and—aspire toward it, for it remains an ideal, a spook. The fetters of reality cut the sharpest welts in my flesh at every moment. But I remain *my own*.[60]

Ownness, first of all, does not mean self-interest or selfishness, since any conception of the "self" can be as much one's own as it can be a spook, a socially produced image of what one *should* be in order to be somebody at all. To be "selfish" is perhaps the most commonplace, banal, and socially acceptable form of behavior there is in capitalist society. The call to "find oneself" or follow one's "true" self fits perfectly well with the neoliberal demands of our era: to cultivate as much human capital as possible for one's prostitution on the market as an extremely precarious, but "self-realized" or "self-fulfilled", wage-slave. To *be yourself* today almost always means adapting one's soul to the needs of the market, or to find oneself reflected in a menu of tailored commodities particularly suited to one's niche identity. All these market-mediated identities are not *my own*, Stirner would say, I am rather their product. Ownness is the complete destitution of these identities and pseudo-selves.[61]

The concept of ownness is also not identical with freedom, at least, not *negative* freedom. To Stirner, freedom is always an external ideal outside my control, never an inner reality starting from my experience. To be free is to be *from*, while to be one's own is to have *power to*. As Stirner suggests in the above quotation, *ownness* refers to my persistent power to maintain, create, or dissolve my I *despite* the immensity of constraints, obligations, rules, norms and images pressed upon me. Freedom is always outside my grasp, since there is always *one more* constraint from which to be free. Ownness is I myself, no matter how deep the "fetters of reality" limit me. To remain *my own* or to be an *owner* is to live according to one's distinct *ownness*. Ownness thus signifies an almost ontological power of self-control, self-fashioning, and self-determination, somewhat similar to Sartre's idea of radical freedom.[62] The distinction between freedom and ownness is consequently not absolute; I will come back to it shortly.

Often translated (wrongly) as *peculiarity*, *personality*, or *characteristic*, Stirner's concept of *Eigenheit* is not a trait or property one *has*, but a form of life one *does*. That is, ownness designates the mode of individual existence that resists capture in alien forms of thought, reified practices, and generic relations. Ownness, in short, is the opposite of alienation. It describes how an owner relates to itself across the abyss of its properties, on its own terms, with its own power. For Stirner, ownness is what remains of oneself when everything sacred, static, and alien has been stripped away. It cannot be known in advance what this means for each individual, since every unique one must determine for themselves who they are to be.

"Ownness does not have any alien standard," Stirner writes, "as it is not in any sense an *idea* like freedom, morality, humanity, and the like: it is only a description of the—owner."[63] If ownness is not a normative idea like freedom, morality and humanity, but a description of the owner, then what about the owner does ownness describe? Although Stirner is not always so clear, I will attempt a few suggestions: ownness describes an owner's inner relation to itself; it marks how an owner consumes its own properties without being consumed in turn; it illustrates the singular content of the *I*—its uniqueness—although there is no essence to it; ownness names the negativity of the owner, its power to dissolve and withdraw from its property at will.

In Hegelian terms, ownness is an *infinite* relation, since it depends on nothing outside itself to be itself. For Hegel, the most familiar example of the infinite self-relation is the *I*. "When we say 'I', that is the expression of the infinite self-relation that is at the same time negative."[64] To say "I" is to infinitely relate oneself to oneself as a singular being that knows itself as self-relating; and yet, to know oneself as "I" is also to posit a negative relation, since it necessarily entails a distinction from others. This infinite, self-relating negativity of the I—seen not from the third-person perspective of observing consciousness, but from the first-person perspective of experience—is what ownness attempts to describe.

"Ownness," Stirner asserts, "is the creator of everything."[65] It is the source of self-creation and self-destruction, that which enables one to become unique out of their various properties, and that which allows one to dissolve their properties back into nothing. It is the power to consume that which consumes you, to destroy that which destroys you. An owner can consume its properties, but never its ownness, for the act of self-dissolution is itself a proof of one's own power. Ownness can never be *given* by another, like a privilege or a right; it can only be *expressed* in one's actions, like a disposition or power.

Stirner's injunction for those who seek to be their own is to give up all sacred property *without* falling into a new faith, a new submission. To renounce alien principles, reified relations, and fixed ideas, however, does not mean abandoning principles, relations and ideas as such. Rather, it means making them one's own, internalizing them, using and abusing them as one's property, one's enjoyment. "Ownness permits everything, even apostasy, defection."[66] When individualism and the supremacy of the ego become ruling dogmas, then the greatest act of ownness is perhaps the apostasy of the I itself.

Heidegger

In addition to Hegel and Sartre, Stirner's concept of ownness resonates across the history of philosophy. For instance, in *Being and Time*, Heidegger describes a phenomenological condition called *mineness* [*Jemeinigkeit*] which, at first glance, appears similar to Stirner's ownness. Mineness just means that, "the being whose analysis our task is, is always we ourselves. The being of this being is always *mine*."[67] For any "Dasein" (Heidegger's jargon for the particular mode of existence for human beings), the question of being always emerges out of one's concern with their own existence, and not as some indifferently present objective genus, waiting to be investigated. "When we speak of Dasein," Heidegger notes, "we must always use the *personal* pronoun along with whatever we say: 'I am,' 'You are.'"[68]

Stirner would agree with this fundamental "mineness" of our existence, but just because *being* is first of all *mine* does not mean that I identify with it, that I *own* it. However, here too Heidegger would concur. To Heidegger, each Dasein has the choice of whether or not to take up its "ownmost possibility", to become its own potential, or to lose itself in the indeterminacy of the many. Heidegger creates a new word to describe this proper mode of being, one uncannily close to Stirner's own neologism of *Eigenheit*: *Eigentlichkeit*, usually translated as "authenticity". For Heidegger, an "authentic" being appropriates its own potentiality, and does not let it waste away in average everydayness or inauthenticity. He writes:

> Dasein *is* always its possibility. It does not 'have' that possibility only as a mere attribute of something objectively present. And because Dasein is always essentially its possibility, it *can* 'choose' itself in its being, it can win itself, it can lose itself, or it can never and only 'apparently' win itself. It can only have lost itself and it can only have not yet gained itself because it is essentially possible as authentic [*eigentliches*], that is, it belongs to itself. The two kinds of being of *authenticity* and *inauthenticity* [*Eigentlichkeit* und *Uneigentlichkeit*]—these expressions are terminologically chosen in the strictest sense of the word—are based on the fact that Dasein is in general determined by always being-mine.[69]

Is Stirner's *Eigenheit* the original template for Heidegger's *Eigentlichkeit*? If so, then Stirner is in trouble, since authenticity is perhaps the weakest element in Heidegger's phenomenological edifice, riven with ideological trappings.[70] Although they overlap at parts, *ownness* and *authenticity* describe different modes of existence. For Heidegger, authenticity refers to Dasein's own capacity to appropriate its potentiality as a fundamentally *temporal* being, concerned with its own finitude, and faced with its destiny. Ownness, however, cares little for being-towards-death, as it only describes the persistent power of an I to overcome its alienation through consumption of everything external, fixed and alien to it. Death too is an abstraction to be consumed, like all others, in my own unique way. Stirner's *Einzige* does not give a shit about being "authentic" or facing up to its historical destiny; those are just more phantoms in the picture gallery of spirits. If enjoying my life in the cellars and bars of depraved proletarians is somehow inauthentic, then authenticity has no value to me. The joy of ownness overrides the tragedy of history.

All things are nothing to me, Stirner writes, even my own destiny.

Foucault

Stirner's thought does not only speak to 20th century philosophical concerns, but also to those of the 1st century. According to Foucault, Stirner's philosophy is a modern reprise of the ancient Stoic precept of "caring for the self". The concept of ownness could then be read as one of the first attempts at reigniting an ethics and aesthetics of the self, a project taken up by many individualist philosophers in the nineteenth-century. For Foucault,

> A whole section of nineteenth century thought can be reread as a difficult attempt, a series of difficult attempts, to reconstitute an ethics and an aesthetics of the self. If you take, for example, Stirner, Schopenhauer, Nietzsche, dandyism, Baudelaire, anarchy, anarchist thought, etcetera, then you have a series of attempts that are, of course, very different from each other, but which are all more or less obsessed by the question: Is it possible to constitute, or reconstitute, an aesthetics of the self? At what cost and under what conditions?[71]

What is an "aesthetics of the self" and how does it relate to Stirner's concept of *ownness*? Stirner's text centers around the question of how one relates to oneself. His diagnosis is that we have not treated ourselves well, that we are sick, alienated from ourselves, stuck in fixed thought patterns and petrified forms of practice. Only a series of consumptive practices of ownness will allow us to come to terms with ourselves again, to liberate ourselves from our self-imposed estrangement. For Stirner, these practices are a kind of ownership of the self. Such ownership requires consuming one's properties so as to bring them back in line with oneself.

Stirner's ownness highlights the power to master one's own

condition even when one cannot master one's own fate. Epictetus, the Hellenistic stoic of the 1st century, made a distinction between things that that are "up to us" and things that are not; the former can be controlled, the latter cannot, and freedom lies in knowing the difference.[72] Similarly, Stirner separates what is our property from what is not. If something is up to me, under my control, then I can consume it as property, and enjoy myself. If it is not my property, not up to me, then it should not matter to my development; it is nothing to me. However, for Stirner, the difference between what is mine and what is not-mine is not some absolute limit, but rather a historically produced boundary, constantly challenged by my own self-activity. To push that limit is to internalize what appears external, to render artificial what seems natural, to make intelligible the opaque, and reappropriate the product of one's own power.

In this sense, Stirner's theory of property is more like a theory of ethical life than a theory of legal rights. It describes the conditions by which one can achieve their own enjoyment. Stirner's formula is not "know thyself" but *own thyself*. This is not meant in a legal or economic sense (as a libertarian might say), but in an ethical sense, as a demand to seize a non-alienated form of life. This requires practice and training, "consumption" and "dissolution." For Foucault, such practices of the self are not simply a kind of self-styling. The relation to oneself is rather the primary register in which contemporary political power operates. To reclaim that power is both indispensable and near impossible. As Foucault says,

> I think we may have to suspect that we find it impossible today to constitute an ethic of the self, even though it may be an urgent, fundamental, and politically indispensable task, if it is true after all that there is no first or final point of resistance to political power other than in the relationship one has to oneself.[73]

Ownness constitutes the fount of self-formation in Stirner. In order to be a unique I, one must resist the tendency towards generality. To Stirner and Foucault, the main mechanism that distributes and imposes generalities on individuals is the *state*. Therefore, to resist the state and form oneself into a unique I are one and the same thing. This is the meeting point between Foucault and Stirner. But whereas Foucault understands the practices of the self as an ethic of freedom, Stirner's ethic of ownness displaces freedom from its pedestal and consumes it as one property among others.

Freedom

As mentioned before, Stirner differentiates his idea of radical ownness from the liberal concept of freedom. One way he illustrates this difference is in how each relates to the individual and its property:

> Freedom teaches only: get rid of yourselves, get rid of everything annoying; it does not teach you who you yourselves are. *Away, away!* Thus sounds its battle cry, and you, eagerly heeding its call, even get rid of yourselves, 'deny yourselves'. But ownness calls you back to yourselves, it says 'come to yourself.' Under the aegis of freedom you get rid of many kinds of things, but something new oppresses you again…As *own* you are *actually rid of everything*, and what clings to you *you have accepted*; it is your choice and your pleasure. The *own* one is the *free-born*, the one free to begin with; the free one, on the contrary, is only the *freedom-addicted*, the dreamer and enthusiast.[74]

For Stirner, freedom is a form of self-denial, a call to get rid of one's attachments and desires, joys and pains, in hope of one day being free from everything, even oneself. Except, there is *always more* to get rid of. Like Hegel's bad infinity, something can always be added to the sequence of oppression. Each oppression creates a new freedom, and each freedom fixes a new identity in order to demand it. One is thus never actually free, only potentially so. Ownness, on the contrary, assumes one's radical freedom from the very beginning, and builds upon it. Only by starting from yourself, Stirner suggests, from your needs and powers, your pleasures and suffering, can you confront all the external and internal constraints against you. Whereas freedom demands recognition from others, ownness takes it for oneself, and consumes it as nothing. To be one's own is to even have the power to *get rid of oneself*, if one so chooses; to wish for freedom is to continuously seek this release from others, like an addict searching for another fix.

Initially, it seems tempting to interpret ownness as a type of freedom, as one way of expressing personal freedom. For Stirner, it is exactly the opposite: *freedom is one way of expressing ownness.* Freedom can be granted or taken, imposed or created; it can be formal or material, collective or individual; it can vary according to social, sexual, political, legal, and economic criteria. None of this really matters to Stirner. What matters is whether any particular kind of freedom is *one's own* or not. That is, it matters whether freedom is an *accomplishment* of one's own activity, and thus a result and expression of ownness, or if it is something *alien*, a result of another's power and thus an expression of one's impotence. In the latter case, freedom appears not as one's own but as an external ideal, a coercive right, an abstract law, a social norm, a moral value—that is, as something else, *separate* from me.

Ownness, after all, describes how an individual relates to its own determinations, including freedom. As noted above, it is not a quality or property, but a mode of self-relation. Freedom, on the other hand, is at best a negative relation to external constraints, and at worst, an ideological weapon used to justify any sacrifice of the individual. In a dialogue with himself, Stirner wonders why freedom is a worthy goal at all:

> Who is it that is to become free? You, I, we. Free from what?
> From everything that is not you, not I, not we. I, therefore, am
> the kernel that is to be delivered from all wrappings and—
> freed from all cramping shells. What is left when I have been
> freed from everything that is not I? Only I, and nothing but
> I. But freedom has nothing to offer to this I itself. As to what
> is now to happen further after I have become free, freedom
> is silent—as our governments, when the prisoner's time is
> up, merely let him go, thrusting him into abandonment. Now
> why, if freedom is striven after for love of the I after all, why
> not choose the I itself as beginning, middle, end?[75]

One should be cautious here, for Stirner is not saying that
freedom is insignificant. He is only questioning its unparalleled
rank in the hierarchy of goods, as well as the means by which
one achieves it. To choose the "I" as beginning, middle, and end
is to decide on how one seeks freedom in the first place, where
it is sought, and to what ends. Ownness orients the generality
of freedom back to the singularity of the individual. This dis-
alienation of freedom is its very consumption. Praising freedom
while ignoring the conditions by which it is realized only
mystifies its power over us. Stirner rather asks, who frees who,
how, and when? Between a vague hope for freedom and a clear
presence of I, Stirner chooses I:

> Am I not worth more than freedom? Am I not the one that
> makes myself free, am not I the first? Even unfree, even in a
> thousand fetters, I still am; and I am not, like freedom, only
> existing in the future and in hopes, but even as the most abject
> slave I am—present.[76]

A slave can be her own while not being free, Stirner claims, whereas a slave not her own can never be free. Ownness thus conditions freedom, determining its proper form as *self-emancipation*. Self-emancipation as the meaning of owned freedom parallels Stirner's earlier discussion of self-empowerment as the meaning of owned property. "All freedom is essentially — *self-emancipation* — that I can have only so much freedom as I procure for myself by my ownness."[77] Freedom in the form of self-emancipation is absolute. Anything besides self-emancipation is only a "particular freedom" and, as Stirner argues, a "piece of freedom is not freedom."[78] There are two meanings of freedom here: one conditioned by ownness and accomplished through acts of self-liberation, and one conditioned by others, accomplished through "petitioning" and granted by "grace."[79] The explicitly political value of Stirner's concepts become clearer here, for not only does he describe different strategies for *becoming free*, but different meanings underlying them as well.

Stirner makes this point through the example of freedom of speech and a free press. This was a crucial political issue for Stirner since his friends, "The Free", were constantly getting arrested, and their work often censored and banned. In fact, Stirner's own book was immediately banned upon publication, but was released a few days later because the Minister of Interior considered it "too absurd to be dangerous."[80] Directly challenging his own persecuted friends, he puts forward the argument that the demand for free speech only furthers one's subjugation. Like property, true freedom cannot be bestowed, only taken. To ask for *permission* to be free is thus absurd, since that renders one's freedom dependent on the grace of another, and thus unfree. Thus, "freedom of the press is only *permission of the press*, and the state never will and never can voluntarily allow me to smash it by means of the press."[81] For speech to be truly free, it must be free *from* the state, not within it. Petitioning for freedom is like asking someone else to eat for you.

Instead of asking for a free press, Stirner provokes us to

occupy it: "*Ownness of the press,* or *property in the press*, that is what I will take."[82] To read this as literally "owning" the press in the capitalist sense of private property is ridiculous, for no matter who legally owns it, the limits of speech are still regulated by the state. Press-ownness means creating one's own means of speech in whatever shape or form, legal or not. To make the press into one's own property is to expropriate it, consume it, negate it and replace it. Freedom is thus achieved only when asking for it becomes irrelevant. "I am not wholly free until I ask about nothing."[83]

In another example, Stirner describes how proletarians in the modern bourgeois state are dependent on capitalists for their income. "But how is it with one who has nothing to lose, how is it with the proletarian? Since he has nothing to lose, he doesn't need state protection for his 'nothing.'"[84] The capitalist state does nothing for the worker, except "suck his blood dry." Wage-labor "is not recognized as to its *value*; it is *exploited*, a *spoil*." The whole "machinery of the state" is poised against workers, biased in favor of the private-property-owning capitalists. Because of their non-possession, proletarians "have nothing to lose" when they revolt. Asking for higher pay in order to "realize" the true value of their labor is absurd, since proletarians already have the "most enormous power *in* their hands."[85] That is, workers have the power to *strike*, to refuse work. But they must recognize this power first, and claim it as their *own*. If only the workers became "conscious of it and used it, nothing would withstand them; they would only have to stop labor, regard the product of labor as theirs, and enjoy."[86] In other words, *class struggle gets the goods.* Proletarians do not emancipate themselves by begging, by compromise and petitions. They get free by recognizing their own power, and acting upon it. To realize this power is at the same time to abolish their own status as powerless, propertyless subjects.

Here once more, Stirner situates power in the hands of those who are subjugated, those who not only *have* nothing, but *need* nothing. Their ownness is the source from which they draw power to realize their value and overturn their alien conditions. This not only means striking from labor, but striking *against* labor as well. And what if the state or capitalist concedes and offers to set you free? Stirner's anti-libertarian response: "The one set free is nothing but a probationer, a *libertinus*, a dog dragging a piece of chain with him: he is an unfree man in the garment of freedom, like the ass in the lion's skin."[87]

Self-Consumption

Out of ownness, the owner consumes its properties, rendering them nothing. That is, it incorporates otherness into itself, and affirms its own power as unique. It seems as though the owner exists both outside *and* inside its own activity of consumption. Outside, since it exists separate from its property, consuming it as its own; inside, since the owner is not grounded by some transcendental ego, but only exists in its activity. Where, then, is the I? Is it a black hole that absorbs everything into itself? Is it a fixed point, an absolute ground, an ontological substance? "The I *is* not all, but *destroys* all," Stirner remarks. "Only the self-dissolving I, the never-being I, the—*finite* I is actually I."[88] The actual, finite I is not a stable ground of action or consumption. Rather, it is *produced* through its consumption, and *consumed* through its production. Produced, since the I emerges out of the singular history of its own consumption. And consumed, because the I dissolves into the temporal stream of its own production. Circulating through production and consumption, Stirner's "self-dissolving I" takes on and discards multiple forms of appearance, but always circles back to the creative nothing at the center of its ownness.

Stirner's use of economic language is no accident, for he takes individuals first of all to be consuming and producing beings, with material wants, bodily desires, and physical needs, and not as autonomous free wills with abstract rights, moral duties, and universal consciousness. Economic relations of property, not ideal categories of right, form the material conditions for life. To gain power over one's life then requires appropriating those conditions, owning them, consuming them, dissolving them, and using them for oneself. It means becoming an owner, not something owned, becoming a unique I, not a generic bearer of alien functions. The unique I, however, must not be confused with its material body and properties; it is never identical with its conditions, but rather expressed through the singular and dynamic process of consuming those conditions.

Neither a formal essence nor a material body, Stirner's I at points resembles the self-mediating power of negativity that Hegel identifies as *spirit* or *Geist*. But whereas Hegel sees the absolute subject-object of *Geist* in the movement of history towards freedom, Stirner sees the end of history in *me*, *this* one, I. To begin from myself means owning these presuppositions of history, these conditions of what I am and what I could be, consuming them, discarding them, becoming something else. Never satisfied with one constellation of property and self, the owner consumes itself as its consumes the world.

In other words, for the owner to remain its own, it must tirelessly ward off its own petrification into something alien, dead. It must dissolve itself whenever it becomes fixed in one form, one identity. That means, it must become food to itself, property to be consumed. How can I become my own property? This is not an economic-legal question but an ethico-political one. Not how can I acquire a property right in myself, but how can I relate to myself such that I remain my own even in the form of another. In Stirner's framework, to become my own property means allowing myself to be consumed by my ownness. It means *letting go* of myself, renouncing my absolute will to be unique, separate from others, for that too traps me into one form of being I. To remain one's own is thus to let go of the will to be only one's own.

Ownness, however, needs no permission to act upon me. It takes, occupies, expropriates and dissolves my I into nothing, so that I can be reborn again, produced and consumed anew. Where does the I fall in this process? This is the wrong question, for the I is not *in* this process, but *is* this process. "That I consume myself, means only that I am."[89] I am an auto-cannibal, eating myself to protect myself from my own loss into something other, something fixed, alien. If I fail to destroy myself on my own terms, then I am destroyed by another. The process by which one loses oneself precisely due to the fact that one attacks one's own defenses can be called *autoimmunity*.

Jacques Derrida described an "autoimmunitary process" as "that strange behavior where a living being, in quasi-*suicidal* fashion, 'itself' works to destroy its own protection, to immunize itself *against* its 'own' immunity."[90] Derrida relates this medical logic to the political procedure behind the event of September 11th, 2001. On a different scale, no less singular, an autoimmunitary logic can be attributed to each and every instance in which an individual loses itself in something alien, some fixed generality it can no longer control or even recognize itself within. For instance, becoming a "citizen", a "worker", or a "human." All these slippages occur against the owner's own internal protection against fixity. These identities (citizen, worker, human) are better conceived as immunities. These immunities supply the backbone to community as opposed to the ownness that defines Stirner's *union* or *association*. Stirner interprets these collapses into alienated identities as self-incurred processes, as the result of one's own failure to consume oneself. Fixed identities are practices of the self that no longer care for itself. Every time I fail to consume myself as property, I reify myself, and acquire an identity. I am no longer I but it.

Right before Stirner walks off stage in the same manner he strutted on (in the clothes of Goethe, announcing "all things are nothing to me"), he restates this paradoxical, ethical injunction. In order to own oneself, one must affirm their own self-negation. In other words, one must acknowledge the finitude of existence not as some ultimate ground of meaning, but as one last property to be consumed: "If I concern myself for myself, the unique one, then my concern rests on its transitory, mortal creator, who consumes himself."[91] The self-consumption of the I is thus not a heroic act of freedom or autonomy but rather a submission to the power of ownness and the dissolution of identity. To be a unique one, concerned only for oneself, is to be nothing, nothing at all.

Nothing

Before this final exit, Stirner distinguishes his positions from that of Feuerbach and Hegel, the philosophical authorities of his time. Stirner opposes himself to them not in order to produce some "third thing that shall 'unite'" all the differences, some synthesis or such.[92] No third party will show the truth behind opposing sides, no common trait or equal point will be shared. As he puts it, "the opposition deserves rather to be *sharpened*."[93] In this sharpening, Stirner coughs up another clue into the cannibalism of the ego:

> Feuerbach, in the *Principles of the Philosophy of the Future*, is always insisting upon *being*. In this, with all his antagonism to Hegel and the absolute philosophy, he too is stuck fast in abstraction; for 'being' is abstraction, as is even 'the I'. Only *I am* not abstraction alone: I *am* all in all, consequently even abstraction or nothing: I am all and nothing; I am not a mere thought, but at the same time I am full of thoughts, a thought-world. Hegel condemns the own, mine [*das Meinige*] — 'opinion' [*Meinung*]. 'Absolute thinking' is that which forgets that it is *my* thinking, that I think, and that it exists only through *me*. But I, as I, devour again what is mine, am its master; it is only my *opinion*, which I can at any moment

change, annihilate, take back into myself, and consume. Feuerbach wants to smite Hegel's 'absolute thinking' with *unconquered being*. But in me being is as much conquered as thinking is. It is *my* being, as the other is *my* thinking.[94]

Foreshadowing Marxist critiques of ideology, poststructuralist critiques of meta-narratives, and standpoint critiques of epistemology, Stirner's claim here is simple. Nominally, it is that Feuerbach's "sensuous" philosophy relies on abstraction as much as Hegel's "absolute" philosophy does. Feuerbach and Hegel, according to Stirner, both reify thought and being, separating them from *me*, the finite owner of thoughts and being. For Stirner, *I* am the living negativity that provides the fuel for idealist and materialist philosophies. Absolute thinking is *my* thought, unthinkable being is *my* being—I am all of them and none of them, for they are mine to use and abuse at will. Being and thought are my predicates, my properties, not my essence or ideal, but merely my food.

How am I "all *and* nothing"? The *all* of the I can be correlated to the ownness of the owner, that which remains even through one's self-consumption. But what about the *nothing* of the I? This nothing is not a simple negation of the all, but rather its very condition. The totality of the I—my property, power, consumption, dissolution, and even ownness—is grounded in nothing. All relations and actions of my I circulate into and out of this nothing. Stirner calls this the "creative nothing, the nothing out of which I myself as creator create everything."[95] This nothing is not empty, but rather the source of the I's ownness. The I is not a thing, it cannot be reduced to a thing, or come from anything. As a singular non-thing, the I can only come from *nothing*. One way to grasp the "creative nothing" out of which the I as creator creates everything is to think of it as *time*. Stirner hints at this when he writes that the true way to become who you are is to "dissolve yourself as time dissolves everything."[96] For time is the non-thing that destroys and gives life to all things, that consumes and produces everything as its own, that annihilates and creates everything out of itself. All things are nothing to me, for I am time, the destroyer of all things.

Stirner gives a proper name to the nothing that is I. As that which has no substance, no distinguishing marks, no differences, it can be named precisely for being *different* in its radical indifference. Absolutely split from all, the nothing is not only singular, but the source of singularity. Anything else is "something", that is, already related to other things. The nothing is that from which ownness emerges. The consumption and dissolution of any thing separate from me as my own property confirms my power, my ownness. Ownness, to Stirner, is not grounded in any other principle; it comes from nowhere, from *nothingness*, no place at all. But this nothingness, due to its radical indifference to all, marks it as singular. As such, this nothingness deserves a proper name, proper because it has no generality.

Stirner's philosophy hinges on this nomination, this proper name for the I: *the Unique* [*Der Einzige*]. The unique is the proper name for the nothing that conditions our being. But this name is also not a name, for any name that can express the nothingness of the I would make it into something, and thus reify it.[97] In his replies to critics, Stirner dwells upon this problem of naming the unique. Writing in the third person, he welcomes this paradox of the unnameable name: "Stirner names the unique and says at the same time that 'names don't name it.' He utters a name when he names the unique, and adds that the unique is only a name... The unique is an expression with which, in all frankness and honesty, one recognizes that he is expressing nothing."[98] Stirner rejects every attempt to fix one's identity through a concept.

To call oneself "unique" is to thus to recognize the lack of self-identity and to acknowledge the impossibility of attributing a fundamental essence to oneself. Instead, Stirner highlights the contingency of any and every property of oneself, whether that be reason, language, mind, sociality, humanity or whatever.

All things are nothing to me, *but yet I am*. The proper name for the nothingness of the I is *Einzige*, or unique. This name communicates without communicating anything. It has no conceptual content, *except* in expressing its emptiness. Stirner wants a concept that communicates non-conceptually, a word that expresses non-linguistically, a name that names non-nominally. The content of the *Einzige* negates the form of its enunciation, and yet this negation is telling of its content. Stirner's dance with nominalism thus comes to a head in proposing a name that names nothing except the unnameability of a singular nothing:

> The unique is a word, and everyone is always supposed to be able to think something when he uses a word; a word is supposed to have thought content. But the unique is a thoughtless word; it has no thought content. So then what is its content, if it is not thought? It is content that cannot exist a second time and so also cannot be expressed, because if it could be expressed, actually and wholly expressed, it would exist for a second time; it would exist in the 'expression.' Since the content of the unique is not thought content, the unique cannot be thought or said; but since it cannot be said, it, this perfect phrase, is not even a phrase.[99]

Since the unique names nothing, it does not even matter that it is just a word, for it is a word used against the tendency to fix its meaning in language. To *be* unique is not to be a word or an idea, but to be oneself, I, this nothing. An I is unique precisely in how it relates to the nothing from which it emerges and towards which it courses. To be a unique one then means attempting to own the nothingness that underlies one's brief existence. In other words, it is to own time.

Levinas

In discussing the relation between two "uniques", Stirner notes:

> The last and most decided opposition, that of unique against
> unique, is at bottom beyond what is called opposition, but
> without having sunk back into 'unity' and unison... The
> opposition vanishes in complete—*severance* or uniqueness.
> This might indeed be regarded as the new point in common
> or a new parity, but here the parity consists precisely in the
> disparity, and is itself nothing but disparity, a par of disparity,
> and that only from him who institutes a 'comparison.'[100]

This confrontation between *unique* and *unique* perfectly captures
the relation between Stirner and Levinas, two wildly different
philosophers whose thought touches at the extremes. Levinas,
the 20th century French phenomenologist, declared that ethics
is first philosophy. As *the* thinker of alterity, he argues for
the ontological primacy of the "other" over oneself. Levinas's
phenomenological analysis of human beings results in the thesis
that each and every human being has an infinite responsibility to
the "other". The infinity of the other is not just posited, according
to Levinas, but concretely *experienced* in the relation between
another and I, particularly through face-to-face interaction.

Between Stirner and Levinas, there appears to be an absolute
contradiction of viewpoints: one privileges the "ego" above all
others and one privileges the "other" above all egos. Yet, it can
be shown that Levinas's thought *complements* Stirner's. Their
disparate starting points allow them to meet on their own terms.
Their differences only mask their proximity.

In the first half of *Totality and Infinity*, published in 1961,
Levinas describes the preconditions for experiencing the infinity
of the other person. He calls this phenomenological condition
separation, complete atheistic egoism, and it forms the initial
break with the concept of *totality*. With his unique syntax,

Levinas writes:

> To separate oneself, to not remain bound up with a totality, is positively to be *somewhere*, in the home, to be economically. The 'somewhere' and the home render egoism, the primordial mode of being in which separation is produced, explicit. Egoism is an ontological event, an effective rending, and not a dream running along the surface of being, negligible as a shadow. The rending of a totality can be produced only by the throbbing of an egoism, that is neither illusory nor subordinated in any way whatever to the totality it tends. *Egoism is life: life from... , or enjoyment.*[101]

The *separated* ego, according to Levinas, loves life and all its singular pleasures. The enjoyment of the ego is guaranteed by its separation from all generalities, by its absolute uniqueness or *unicity*, as Levinas calls it. "This logically absurd structure of unicity, this non-participation in genus," Levinas claims, "is the very egoism of happiness."[102] The separated ego *enjoys* not only its life, but its *possessions* as well, for in its possessions it confirms its self once more.

With this brief description, it is easy to see the connection between Stirner and Levinas. In short, Stirner's philosophy articulates the condition of possibility for Levinas's ethics. The *Einzige* describes a radical separation, the negation of totality, that which refuses to be thematized or subsumed under any fixed concept. The individual—the owner, unique, I—is life expressed as enjoyment, or as Stirner calls it, *self-enjoyment*.

Levinas's critical modification is to claim that this egoism of the ego, this anarchic I, is still too autarchic. Completely free to be what its ownness desires, Stirner's ego is its own master. This means that the ownness of the I, even when incomprehensible or unintelligible to me, is still *mine*. The creative negativity that consumes gods, man and worlds as its property, that births the uniqueness of the owner from nothing, is inescapably bound to my will. Ownness, in other words, always refers back to me. This circle between the ego and its own, between the unique and its property, treats the power of ownness as a property of the contingent I. In attempting to free ownness by situating it in the empty core of one's self, however, Stirner sinned against his own axiom: "If they nevertheless give you freedom, they are simply rogues who give you more than they have. For then they give you nothing of their own, but stolen goods: they give you your own freedom, the freedom that you must take for yourselves."[103] To be truly one's own, the site of ownness should be displaced from oneself. If it remains within my I, then I cannot truly *own* it, for it was never *taken*, seized, expropriated. Ownness must come from the outside. To Levinas, this outside is the *other*. Ownness, therefore, comes from the experience of the other.

Without Stirner's *Einzige*, the infinite relation to the other would always be blocked by a given mediation. The total secession from similarity through absolute difference and unicity rightly dissolves both comparison and unity. By shattering every fetter of generality, Stirner's separated I can only be related to another through an absolute relation, an infinite one. For Levinas, the concretely experienced infinite relation is the *ethical* relation to the other.

The location of the origin of ownness is the difference that distinguishes Levinas from Stirner. Levinas shifts the site across the abyss of two singular individuals. This other unique one, the neighbor, communicates *my* ownness through the lens of their face. To a Levinasized Stirner, the infinite experience of the other counts as an experience of unowned ownness. Perhaps this explains the seeming paradox of why two philosophers whose philosophical projects center around diametrically opposed points—Stirner's *I* vs. Levinas's *Other*—are often described with the same adjective: *anarchic*.[104]

Unique

The unique has the power to consume all and be consumed in the process. This annihilating drive is not just negation or nihilism, but the full consumption of life. Stirner asks, "How does one use life?" Answering himself, he declares: "In using it up, like the candle, which one uses in burning it up. One uses life, and consequently himself the living one, in *consuming* it and himself. *Enjoyment of life* is using life up."[105] There is no authentic self to realize, no essence to reveal or identity to defend. There is only the singular experience of consuming life to its end. "The question runs not how one can acquire life, but how one can squander, enjoy it; or, not how one is to produce the true self in himself, but how one is to dissolve himself, to live himself out."[106]

The drive to *live oneself out*, to dissolve oneself in the process of life, is a threat to anything that seeks to remain solid, stable in its identity. What wants to remain solid? Fixed ideas, spooks, gods, states, law, morality, truth, humanity—that whole gambit of alienated powers encountered in the first part of *Der Einzige*. These alienated properties constantly struggle to solidify the negativity of the owner into an identity, to wrest the uniqueness away from the I, to generalize it, capture it, control it. Stirner labels this process *policing*, more specifically, the *police-care* of the state.

Like Foucault a century later, Stirner claims that the police function of the state is not merely to coerce individuals, but to *care* for them. The state "presumes the worst about each one, and takes care, *police-care*, that 'no harm happens to the state.'"[107] Police-care is the taming of one's life through one's own self-repression. It is the creation of "spies" and "secret police" in all of us.[108] Police-care of the self can also be expressed through one's *political* identification with the state: "Anyone in whose head or heart both the *state* is seated, anyone possessed by the state, or the *believer in the state*, is a politician, and remains such to all eternity."[109]

If the state is just a fixed idea, then will its consumption make it disappear? If I do not treat the state as an independent power over me, does it vanish? According to Marx, Stirner believes this to be the case, and thus, he is a fool. In *The German Ideology*, Marx writes,

> On the contrary, now that he [Stirner] no longer looks at the world through the spectacles of his fantasy, he has to think of the practical interrelations of the world, to get to know them and act in accordance with them. By destroying the *fantastic* corporeality which the world had for him, he finds its real corporeality outside his fantasy. With the disappearance of the *spectral* corporeality of the Emperor, what disappears for him is not the corporeality, but the *spectral character* of the Emperor, the actual power of whom he can now at least appreciate in all its scope.[110]

Derrida punctuates this in *Specters of Marx*: "When one has destroyed a phantomatic body, the real body remains."[111] But what constitutes this "real" body? Work, labor, the "practical interrelations of the world." One must now begin the work of mourning, the real work, factory work, production. For Derrida, this *practical* delaying and deferring of the ego's fullness in its consumption constitutes Marx's critical incision into the heart of Stirner's project. For Marx, the consumption and dissolution of abstractions, ideologies and specters forms merely the preconditions for the real labor of materialist critique. Serious critique looks at the social, political, and historical conditions of production, not their reflection in idealist philosophy.

According to Marx, Stirner is a *pre-materialist* thinker. This is not convincing. In *Der Einzige*, Stirner sketches the practical obstructions that block the consumption of reified ideas and alienated relations: money, religion, law, power, police, submission, petition, vanity, addiction. In so doing, he does not provide the first step of materialist critique of social relations, but the *last*. In other words, Stirner should not be read as a pre-materialist thinker, ignoring the "practical interrelations of the world". Neither should he be read as a *materialist* philosopher, centering his analysis solely on historical relations of production. Rather, he should be interpreted as *post-materialist*. That is, Stirner assumes the necessity of materialist analysis as a prior condition for the consumption and dissolution of reified ideas and alienated relations.

When the real body is destroyed, the phantom body remains — that is Stirner's rebuff to Marx. Ideologies outlast their function, identities survive their origin, even economic systems carry on like zombies after they collapse. In attacking this *particular* establishment, that *specific* state or master, one unwittingly sets up another form of domination in the process. And this is not by chance. For Stirner, "the craving for a *particular* freedom always includes the purpose of a new *domination*."[112] This is why he favored social insurrection over political revolution; the former breaks with the form of rule, the latter only the content. The "progressive" transitions from Christianity to humanism, from monarchy to law, from slavery to work are all just a "change of masters" from one kind of rule to the next.[113] The form outlasts the content, and so it too must be emptied.

State

If Stirner's work is supplementary to materialist critique, then what is the status of those forms of alienated property which the unique dissolves in the process of its consumption? At their base, Stirner calls them "fixed ideas", and one iteration of them is the "state." But if the state as idea can only be consumed once we work through the materiality of its domination, then maybe a reversal of privileging needs to occur. The state should not be seen as one of many fixed ideas, but rather *fixed ideas* should be seen as one form of the *state*, as one *state-form*.

There is a reason why Stirner repeatedly focuses on the relation between the individual and the state, and not between the individual and other forms of alienation. The state's conditioning of the individual as subject—*vegetating in subjection*, as Stirner puts it—provides the primary education for revolt. The experience of state-subjection enables one to confront fixed ideas, moralities, truths, and all other types of alienated property and ruling principles. If the *nothing* is the source of singularity, then the *state* is the seed of generality: "Every I is from birth already a criminal against the people, the state ... The unrestrained I—and this we originally are, and in our secret inward parts we remain so always—is the never-ceasing criminal in the state."[114] The state formalizes fixed ideas, and dominates through them. Thus, every unique I must come up against the limits of the state. The unique nothing, the *Einzige*, consumes this power, and annihilates its false pretenses.

Stirner defines the state-form as a mode of structured *dependency*: "What one calls a state is a tissue and network of dependence and adherence; it is a *belonging together*, a binding together, in which those who are placed together fit themselves to each other, or in short, mutually depend on each other: it is the *order* of this *dependence*."[115] The state is an order of dependence, a *tissue*, providing both cohesion and stability for the individual. Ideas are spectral not because they have taken on corporeal form, but because their corporeality has doubled, from state-form to thought-form. Stirner describes this doubling as the "state in the state," or *hierarchy*. But the *unique* consumes this as if it was nothing: "I am the annihilator of its existence, since in the creator's realm it no longer forms a realm of its own, not a state in the state, but a creature of my creative—thoughtlessness."[116]

Another *state in the state* is the political party. Stirner criticizes the party-form as well as its goals: "The party is nothing but a state in the state, and in this smaller bee-state 'peace' will also rule just as in the greater."[117] The bee-state is a reference to his earlier metaphor of the bees who, even when they join together — as Kropotkin meticulously describes in *Mutual Aid* — remain *bees* nonetheless, that is, *subjects* to a queen. The formation of a "free" people doubles this, only forming a new state-in-the-state.

Liberalism, police-care, humanism, Christianity, the party — all these state-forms work to generalize the unique and distribute its singularity across a field of abstractions. Their presence suffocates me, steals the unicity of my nothingness and replaces it with its own. The victor of this struggle is called the *truth*: "Their truth, therefore, is you, or is the nothing which you are for them and in which they dissolve: their truth is their *nothingness*."[118] Overcoming their truth means reappropriating truth as one's own, killing it so that it may live again for oneself. Prefiguring Nietzsche here, Stirner claims that the materiality of truth is more a question of health than a question of fact:

> The truth is dead, a letter, a word, a material that I can use up. All truth by itself is dead, a corpse; it is alive only in the same way as my lungs are alive — namely, in the measure of my own vitality. Truths are material, like vegetables and weeds; as to whether vegetable or weed, the decision lies in me.[119]

Like all properties, truth relates to the health and power of an individual. It is affective, and gives us *enjoyment*. Spinoza describes this as the third form of knowledge, that knowledge which is indistinguishable from the feeling of joy and the creation of power. Spinoza, Stirner, and Nietzsche form a discrete union in their views on truth, power, joy and individuality. There is already much research on Spinoza and Nietzsche, but perhaps it is now time to splice Stirner in between.

Landauer

How do we consume Stirner and not let his thinking become stale?

This problem opens up the question of Stirner's influence, of his legacy in philosophy and psychology, his spectral presence in the shadows of existentialism, communism, anarchism, fascism, and capitalism, all of which Stirner has been associated with or accused of at one point or another.[120]

To take up just one of his many owners, I want to focus on Gustav Landauer, the Jewish, anarchist mystic of fin de siècle Germany. At one point in his life, Landauer, along with anarchist Erich Mühsam and others, took over Munich for three weeks in the infamous Bavarian Soviet Republic (April 6th to May 3rd, 1919), before it was crushed by forty thousand armed troops of the Weimar Republic. An influence on Buber, Benjamin, and Scholem, Landauer's life and work has been nearly forgotten. Like Emma Goldman and other anarchists of the time, Landauer was fascinated by Max Stirner and saw in him a strange prophet whose ideas helped shape his heretical socialism.

On October 26th, 1901, in the newspaper *Die Zukunft*, Landauer published "Anarchic Thoughts on Anarchism."[121] This article criticizes the anarchists of his day. "These anarchists are not anarchic enough for me. They still act like a political party."[122] They are "certainly dogmatists,"[123] their *spook* lies in believing "that one can—or must—bring anarchism to the world; that anarchy is an affair of all humanity; that there will indeed be a day of judgment followed by a millennial era. Those who want 'to bring freedom to the world'—which will always be *their* idea of freedom—are tyrants, not anarchists."[124]

Humanity, anarchy, freedom—spooks! Freedom cannot be *given*, it must be taken, owned. And not simply by violent attacks or peaceful petitions. "The old opposition between destruction and construction begins to lose its meaning: what is at stake are new forms that have never been."[125] These new forms are not to be *longed* for, hoped for, waited for—that is all too Christian for Stirner, and Landauer as well: "Anarchy is not a matter of the future; it is a matter of the present. It is not a matter of making demands; it is a matter of how one lives."[126] What does it mean, then, to live? How should one become an individual? Landauer writes,

> To me, someone without a master, someone who is free, an individual, an anarchist, is one who is his own master, who has unearthed the desire that tells him who he truly wants to be. This desire is his life. The way to heaven is narrow. The way to a newer, higher form of human society passes by the dark, fatal gate of our instincts and the *terra abscondita* — the 'hidden land' — of our soul, which is our world. This world can only be constructed from within. We can discover this land, this rich world, if we are able to create a new kind of human being through chaos and anarchy, through unprecedented, intense, deep experience. Each one of us has to do this. Once this process is completed, only then will anarchists and anarchy exist, in the form of scattered individuals, everywhere. And they will find each other. But they will not kill anyone except themselves — in the mystical sense, in order to be reborn after having descended into the depths of their soul.[127]

To become a free individual is to kill the master in oneself, consuming and dissolving oneself in the process. It means finding one's ownness and finding others who have found their ownness as well. This is how one singularizes life, gives it a meaning and power from which to connect to others as something *more* than just a particular member of a generality, but instead as a universal singularity. "They will find each other," Landauer writes with assurance. Only through an "unprecedented, intense, deep experience" of "chaos and anarchy" can individuals birth a new world, together. These "scattered individuals" do not resign themselves to isolation, apathy or nihilism, but throw themselves into the fire of life, burning every last instant up.

To understand Landauer's appropriation of Stirner, one needs to know a little bit about Jewish mysticism. In the mystical branch of Judaism known as Lurianic Kabbalah, God does not simply create the world out of nothing. Rather, as infinite, it must first *contract itself*, limit itself to make room for nothingness, emptiness. Only in this emptiness can it create something, can it bring forth creations from itself. Through its withdrawal, or *tsimtsum*, it allows space for creation. In exile from itself, God then pours its divine essence into ten vessels or *Sephirot* which can receive and transmit its infinite light in various shades. But these vessels are too fragile to contain the light, they break open, shattering the divine essence into scattered sparks across the universe. The shattering of the vessels, *shevirat ha-kelim*, produces chaos. According to Gerschom Scholem:

> Nothing remains in its proper place. Everything is somewhere else. But a being that is not in its proper place is in exile. Thus, since that primordial act, all being has been a being in exile, in need of being led back and redeemed. The breaking of the vessels continues into all the further stages of emanation and Creation; every thing is in some way broken, everything has a flaw, everything is unfinished. [128]

In exile, the scattered sparks of the divine mingle with the material world. They are trapped, waiting for release. Only through individual human acts of *tikkun*, repairing or mending, can the world be redeemed.[129] But this "redemption is no longer looked upon as a catastrophe, in which history itself comes to an end, but as the logical consequence of a process in which we are all participants."[130] Landauer fuses this mystical anarchism with Stirner's savage "egoism" in order to create something uniquely his own.[131] For Stirner, I consume the world by dissolving my relation to property, and releasing my ownness, my nothingness: "I, this nothing, will bring forth my *creations* from myself."[132] Landauer lyrically translates the power of self-consuming ownness into forms of self-negating tikkun:

One acts with others; one purses municipal socialism; one support farmers', consumers', and tenants' cooperatives; one creates public gardens and libraries; one leaves the cities and works with spade and shovel; one organizes and educates; one simplifies one's material life for the sake of spiritual luxury; one struggles for the creation of new school and new forms of education. However! None of this will really bring us forward if it is not based on a new spirit won by the conquest of one's inner self. We are all waiting for something great – something new. All of our art bears witness to the anxiety involved in preparing for its arrival. But what we are waiting for can only come from ourselves, from our own being. It will come once we force the unknown, the unconscious, up into our spirit; it will come once our spirit loses itself in the spiritless psychological realms that await us in the caverns of our souls. This marks our renewal as human beings, and it marks the arrival of the world we anticipate. Mere intervention in the public sphere will never bring this world about. *It is not enough for us to reject conditions and institutions; we have to reject ourselves.*[133]

All these acts of resistance and creation, of destruction and construction, are wrecked upon the anxiety and anticipation of the world to come. But this world will never just arrive, it can only be *produced*. This production of the unknown, this forced renewal of the unconscious, does not emerge through political *intervention*, but through self-negation. For we ourselves are the broken vessels, and we must break ourselves once more in order to repair the world. One must be prepared to be consumed in the process. For Landauer, the revolutionary task is not to organize the future step by step, but to release it from the strictures of the present into the freedom of uncertainty. Redemption runs through the narrow gate of self-annihilation, in which one's fixed identity as *I, you*, or *we* is reborn in new modes of being and new forms of relating:

> 'Do not kill others, only yourself'–such will be the maxim
> of those who accept the challenge to create their own chaos
> in order to discover their most authentic and precious inner
> being and to become one with the world in a mystical union.
> What these human beings will be able to bring to the world
> will be so extraordinary that it will seem to have come from
> a world altogether unknown. Whoever brings the lost world
> in himself to life–to individual life–and whoever feels like a
> true part of the world and not as a stranger: he will be the
> one who arrives not knowing where from, and who leaves
> not knowing where to. To him the world will be what he is
> to himself. They will live among each other in common – as
> belonging together. This will be anarchy. It might be a distant
> goal. However, we have already come to the point where life
> seems without reason if we do not aim for the unconceivable.
> Life means nothing to us if it is not an infinite sea promising
> eternity. Reforms? Politics? Revolution? It is always more of
> the same. Anarchism? What most anarchists like to present to
> us as an ideal society is too often merely rational and stuck in
> our current reality to serve as a guiding light for anything that
> could or should ever be in the future. Only he who accounts
> for the unknown gives an adequate account, for the true life,
> and the human beings that we truly are, remain unnamed
> and unknown. Hence, not war and murder – but rebirth.[134]

"Do not kill others, only yourself": this is Landauer's ethical
reading of Stirner's call to uniqueness. Landauer does not care
about this reform or that law; even ideal utopias are nothing but
rational extensions of the present, and thus do not truly escape
it. For life to become an "an infinite sea promising eternity," it
can no longer be determined by wage-labor, above all. To bring
the "lost world" in oneself to life will require new forms of

belonging together and living together, forms yet unnamed and unknown, perhaps even unconceivable.

Landauer's mystical appropriation of Stirner is completely his own. He turns Stirner into food for nourishment. Stirner reminds his readers: "For me you are nothing but—my food, just as I too am fed upon and consumed by you."[135] This is not reading or writing for the purpose of truth or accuracy. Indeed, as Stirner puts it, "to do the truth a service is in no case my intent; to me it is just nourishment for my thinking head, as potatoes are for my digesting stomach, or a friend for my social heart."[136]

Against reform, revolution, resignation and isolation, Landauer's communism or anarchy is primarily ethical. Its task is to foster the rebirth of the unique, the singular, the contingent—whether as I or we, but most of all *now*. Like Stirner, Landauer does not demand anything from society. He does not propose a strategy to realize communism in some distant future but describes a condition to cultivate in our lives today. This condition is freedom:

> What I am advocating here is by no means a demand to human society... I demand nothing; I only want to describe the inner condition from which individuals may perhaps come to exemplify communism and anarchy for others. All I want to make clear is that this freedom can only come to life in ourselves and must be nurtured in ourselves before it can appear as an external actuality.[137]

On May 2nd, 1919, the Bavarian Republic was smashed and Landauer was killed. His final words, said to his captors as they killed him: *To think that you are human.* In Stirner's framework, Landauer was beyond human, for he consumed his humanity as well.

Union

How do I relate to another I without sacrificing my uniqueness? Stirner does not think that ideas like "respect" or "love" are useful in guiding the interaction between individuals. Such Christian values have no place in Stirner's universe. Instead, he highlights the *reversibility of violation* captured in his idiosyncratic view of property. Formally similar to Fichte and Hegel, Stirner makes reciprocal recognition key in the relation between unique individuals. But this is not the recognition of personhood, or *freedom*, but of the mutual power for violation, consumption, and expropriation.

Remember, the "right" to property lies in its openness to mutual violation by all. This is not the same as the right to private property nor the public right to the commons. It is rather an openness towards bilateral consumption. Equality, according to Stirner, emerges in the dissolution of comparison through the sharpening of difference. This equality manifests itself in consuming and being consumed by another, in their mutual recognition of one another's power of annihilation. One's *own* property should be defended of course, but if you take it, enjoy! In fact, I'll even smile about it afterwards.[138]

Stirner calls the relation of mutual violation that takes place in between individuals an *association*, *coalition*, or *union* [*Verein*] of Is. This kind of association forms out of the dissolution of state and society, the consumption of their reified forms. In the political state, individuals are not recognized as unique Is but as generic persons, or "human beings". A "society of human beings" is not based on the dynamic, mutual recognition between I and thou, as in a "union of Is", but on alienated, moral rules for obedient subjects.[139] Such a social formation, according to Stirner, is incompatible with truly "egoistic" relations, that is, relations in which individuals appear as singular to each other, and not as bearers of fixed identities, roles, or occupations. Accordingly: "'Human society' is wrecked on the egoists; for they no longer relate to each other as *human beings*, but appear egoistically as an *I* against a completely different and opposed you and yours."[140] Stirner's claim here is that when social relations are already mediated through reified categories like "human being" (or "person", "bourgeois", "proletarian", "citizen"), then *who* one concretely is no longer matters, it is irrelevant, for the way to relate to each other is already determined through the social norms attached to the identities fixed in the categories. Such identities may appear subjectively false, but they function as objectively real. For these "categories" are not just abstractions posited in individual minds but are organizing principles of social intercourse; they are determinate forms of interaction that effectively subsume the content of individual life into a predigested social mechanism with its own laws of motion. The so-called "egoists", however, wreck this social machine by treating one other as *I* and *I* and *I*, that is, as unique, concrete, singular. To be a "human", "worker", "mother", "student", or "citizen" interferes with being myself, and so I prefer not to. Perhaps in the morning I am this, in the afternoon I am that, and in the evening, I am not I at all. I am you or we or a completely other form of belonging, but that is up to me and my accomplices to figure out.

The word *egoist* makes sense in Stirner's time as a provocative rebuke to the hypocritical demands of a self-sacrificing morality based in Christianity; but it no longer holds today. For today the "egoist" is the moral actor *par excellence*, the one who follows all the rules of the economy to maximize their self-interest and gain. The egoist is the paradigm of *homo economicus*, the economic human that seeks profit as producer and marginal utility as consumer, the self-entrepreneur, the self-exploiting manager of one's own capital. As the unchosen envelope for modern individuality, the "egoist" must be consumed along with the state and economy as forms of abstract domination.

To treat others as singular beings can no longer be called *egoistic* in earnest, but rather communistic or anarchistic, maybe even, surprisingly, humanistic. To Marx, the beings whose social relations of production do not dominate them as alienated forms, and who are able to relate to each other as they are and not through character-masks, are called *social individuals*.[141] It does not matter what it is called. The point is that such modes of activity and forms of belonging are contradictory with the present state of affairs. To Stirner, no political, legal, or economic reform can break the fundamental alienation of the state. This requires abolishing the present form of society as we know it and forming free associations of social individuals in its place. As he writes: "We two, the state and I, are enemies. I, the egoist, have not at heart the welfare of this 'human society', I sacrifice nothing to it, I only utilize it; but to be able to utilize it completely, I transform it rather into my property and my creation; that is, I annihilate it, and form in its place the *Union of Egoists*."[142]

What distinguishes this *union* from the state? First, it depends on whether or not one can relate to it as a product of one's own activity, that is, as a reflection of oneself, and second, whether or not one can dispose of it freely, that is, abandon, waste, or destroy it. The union of Is is the creation that reflects the creator, the association that expresses the associators. In that sense, Stirner's union embodies Hegel's concept of freedom as the mode of being with oneself in another [*Beisichselbstsein in einem Anderen*], or *being at home in another*.[143] In an association of free individuals, a union of Is, a commune, or whatever one wants to call it, I am not limited by others, but find myself empowered by them, released from my own limitations. But this does not mean that our interactions are settled once and for all, fixed in a new organizational structure. On the contrary, any social form is but a means to develop the content of each individual, and if it becomes constraining, then it can be dissolved, and developed anew.

Conjoining individuals together into a union concretely overcomes the loss of oneself in fixed ideas, alienated relations, property addictions, object fixations, and so on. By recognizing myself in the other and the other in myself, my capacity to consume that which consumes me grows infinitely. For Hegel, this is the meaning of true freedom *in the state*: "Only in this freedom is the will completely *with itself* [*bei sich*], because it has reference to nothing but itself, so that every relationship of *dependence* on something *other* than itself is thereby eliminated."[144] For Stirner, this is the power of unified ownness *against the state*:

> The difference between state and union is great enough. The former is an enemy and murderer of *ownness*, the latter a son and co-worker of it; the former a spirit that would be adored in spirit and in truth, the latter my work, my product; the state is the lord of my spirit, who demands faith and prescribes to me articles of faith, the creed of legality; it exerts moral influence, dominates my spirit, drives away my *I* to put itself in its place as 'my true I'—in short, the state is *sacred*, and as against me, the individual human being, it is the true human being, the spirit, the ghost; but the union is my own creation, my creature, not sacred, not a spiritual power above my spirit, as little as any association of whatever sort.[145]

Whereas a union is a product of ownness, the state is a producer of alienation. A union is my property, but I am the property of the state. If the state is sacred, then a union is its desecration. A union expands my I into a We; the state contracts my I into It.

Given such bold and broad theses, Stirner's characterization of the state cannot simply be identified with the *political* state. It is rather the entire sphere of politics itself, the realm which divides one against oneself, producing pseudo-divisions of public and private, male and female, citizen and alien, identity and activity, work and leisure, life and economy.[146] Stirner's concept of the "state" is thus perhaps closer to Guy Debord's idea of "spectacle"—for spectacle describes a self-mediating *totality* of social alienation.

Like Marx and Freud before him, Debord is a post-Feuerbachian thinker, and thus shares certain themes with Stirner as well. As Feuerbach appropriated and developed ideas from Hegel, so have Stirner, Marx, Freud and Debord appropriated, criticized and developed Feuerbach's insights on alienation, inversion and projection in their own ways.

According to Debord, *spectacle* names the society in which "all that once was directly lived has become mere representation."[147] In Stirner's framework, Debord is describing a social condition in which individuals can no longer act according to their ownness, but are constrained by the mediations of self-produced spirits, spooks and aliety. In *Society of the Spectacle*, Debord develops this concept dialectically through a series of theses on the commodity, alienation, time, space, history, ideology, and revolution. In the following excerpts, Debord presents spectacle as a form of generalized separation, a structure of alienation, and an ideological negation of life. In so doing, Debord aligns himself with Stirner in a ruthless critique of modern society:

> Separation is the alpha and omega of the spectacle... The spectacle's function in society is the concrete manufacture of alienation... The spectacle appears at once as society itself, as a part of society and as a means of unification. As a part of society, it is that sector where all attention, all consciousness, converges. Being isolated — and precisely for that reason — this sector is the locus of illusion and false consciousness; the unity it imposes is merely the official language of generalized separation... The spectacle is the acme of ideology, for in its full flower it exposes and manifests the essence of all ideological systems: the impoverishment, enslavement and negation of real life.[148]

Stirner would disagree with none of this—as long as one replaces *spectacle* with *state*. Of course, for Debord, spectacle does *not* refer to the state, but to the economy as a totality. The spectacle is the outcome and goal of the dominant mode of production (§6), the fulfilment of commodity fetishism (§36), money's modern aspect (§49), the accumulation of capital to the point of becoming image (§34). Influenced by the Hegelian-Marxism of Lukács, Debord understands the capitalist economy in a very broad sense as a whole system of reified social relations that reproduces subjects, objects and their mediation through value in a particularly inverted manner.[149] Consequently, the state does not *bring about* this process, but rather reflects it ideologically and reinforces it through law and violence. For Stirner, *as for Hegel*, the system of wage-labor and capital is but one sub-set of alienation within the overarching nest of the state. Although Debord and Marx reverse the polarity, even Debord recognizes that the spectacle "is inseparable from the modern State, which, as the product of the social division of labor and the organ of class rule, is the general form of all social division."[150]

The justification of the modern state and economy are usually founded upon an argument about the "state of nature", a mythical time of individualistic chaos and violence that humans had to leave in order to secure peace and stability. By leaving the state of nature behind, individuals gave up isolation for society, freedom for security. Yet to Stirner, and contrary to many caricatures about his "egoism", society *precedes* individuals, binding them in all sorts of relations of dependency from birth onwards. For Stirner, "society is our state of nature."[151] To leave this "society" behind does not entail founding a new state or becoming a hermit, but rather forming a *union of Is*, organizing an association of free individuals, building the commune. The task, therefore, is not to form ties, but to *break* them, since the ties we have are mediated through the state and economy, and thus, are alienations of owned relations, not productions of self- or collective-determination. Breaking social ties allows us to associate ourselves freely and create new forms of intercourse. These new forms of interaction must remain dynamic, alive, attuned to the needs and wills of those who create them, lest they too become petrified—like parties, sects, or other rackets. As Stirner writes:

> The dissolution of *society* is *intercourse* or *union*. A society does assuredly arise by union too, but only as a fixed idea arises by thought, namely, by removing the energy of thought, thinking itself—this restless cancellation of all self-solidifying thoughts—from the thought. If a union has crystallized into a society, then it has ceased to be a unification; for unification is a ceaseless unifying; if it has become a unitedness, come to a standstill, degenerated into a fixity; it is—*dead* as union, it is the corpse of the union or unification, it is—society, community. A striking example of this kind is the *party*.[152]

Unions or associations form the basis of *intercourse*, the movement of power between individuals, and the crafting of new individualities, or what Spinoza calls *composites*. According to the interpretation put forth here, it is justified to call the union of individuals *an individual* as well. This is Stirner's ambivalence, which I think can only be resolved by seeing the *individual* through the Spinozist lens we articulated earlier —as a relation or ratio of power. As a relation of power, the individual is not defined by its parts, but by the *unicity* of its force. The parts are nothing to Spinoza, as property is nothing to Stirner. An individual's ownness is woven from the *composition of forces* or *union of uniques*. Stirner lends credence to this interpretation in the following passage:

> And if I can use him, I doubtless come to an understanding and *make myself at one with him*, in order, by the agreement, to strengthen *my power*, and by combined force to accomplish more than individual force could effect. In this combination, I see nothing but a *multiplication of my force*, and I will keep it only

so long as it is *my* multiplied force. But thus it is a—union.[153]

To "make myself at one with him" is to form a joint body, a unique-of-many, an individual-of-individuals. Spinoza's ontology grants individual status to such a "union of bodies" as composites. We get the core definition in *Ethics*, Book II, proposition 13:

> When a number of bodies, whether of the same or of different size, are so constrained by other bodies that they lie upon another, or if they so move, whether with the same degree or different degrees of speed, that they *communicate their motions* to each other in a certain fixed manner, we shall say that those bodies are united with one another and that they all together *compose one body or individual*, which is distinguished from the others by this *union of bodies*.[154]

Insurrection

The union creates itself as an individual in the same way that an owner appropriates its individuality. Three steps mark this process: *education, secession* and *insurrection*. Education is one way of unlearning fixed ideas, and disalienating oneself. Himself an educator, Stirner writes pedagogically, performatively. His prose provokes, parodies, and mocks the ruling ideas of the day. In so doing, he shows the reader how to do the same. Before writing *Der Einzige*, Stirner wrote a scathing critique of the education system of his time. In "The False Principle of Our Education" (1842), Stirner criticized the creation of "authoritarian" personalities and "submissive creatures", a century before the Frankfurt School. Education should not seek to become "practical", he claims, but free:

> But even practical education still stands far behind personal and free education, and gives the former the skill to fight

through life, thus the latter provides the strength to strike the spark of life out of oneself; if the former prepares one to find oneself at home in a given world, so the latter teaches one to be at home with oneself. We are not yet everything when we move as useful members of society; we are much more able to perfect this only if we are free human beings, self-creating (creating ourselves) persons.[155]

Prefiguring his notion of the unique, Stirner concludes that only the self-dissolution of fixed and frozen knowledge can give birth to a free personality: "*Knowledge* must die in order to be resurrected as *will* and create itself anew each day as a free *person*."[156] In *Der Einzige*, he reiterates this point by describing the necessity for self-education, education as liberation into ownness, noting that "our whole education is calculated to produce *feelings* in us, impart them to us, instead of leaving their production to ourselves however they may turn out."[157]

Secession is the movement by which one subtracts from the bonds of the state. "All states, constitutions, churches, have sunk by the *secession* of individuals."[158] This is not protest or revolution, but the refusal to even engage: disengagement, withdrawal, strike, evasion. Secession occurs when individuals block the reproduction of everyday life. Unions, associations, and communes are formed from seceded individuals, those who do not seek to form a new state or society, but to coexist together in dissolution. Giorgio Agamben, in *The Coming Community* of 1990, makes no progress from Stirner when he writes about the politics to come: "What the State cannot tolerate in any way, however, is that the singularities form a community without affirming an identity, that humans co-belong without any representable condition of belonging."[159] He bases this claim on Alain Badiou's argument in *Being and Event* concerning the real foundation of the state. There, Badiou argues that "the State is not founded upon the social bond, which it would express, but rather the un-binding, which it prohibits."[160] Or, in Agamben's words, it is founded upon *dissolution*.[161]

Stirner's idea of secession or *exit* goes further than Agamben's "co-belonging without representation" and Badiou's "un-binding." For Stirner, one dissolves the relation to the state by entering into a union, association or commune. The union is an instrument to be used, owned; it is nothing beyond the use one makes of it. If one must be faithful to the union at all costs, then the function of the union has been displaced by the principle of state. The union is not a pool into which all seceded individuals gather. There is no single union, only a plurality of free associations, unions of unions which can even act as a single force when working in concert. But the logic of secession or exit functions there too. Secession is not only valid in relation to the state, but to what one exits *into* as well. Secession works all the way down, and everything one unbinds into can itself be unbound. If not, then the state has trickled-down as well. This absolute logic of secession, of seceding from the seceded, is central to *owning* oneself and the union. Just as no property that I cannot destroy can ever be my own, no union that cannot be dissolved will ever be our own. If a union of *I*s or association of individuals cannot dissolve itself, then it has hardened beyond its purpose into something alien, dead. Neither should my representation of myself nor my stagnant union dominate my restless activity of consumption and destruction of property. When I become a fixed idea to myself, alien to my own activity, or when my association becomes an empty shell of interaction, just another form of work, then there is no need to keep on being who I think I am or to keep on uniting with others in this particular way. There is no need to retain members in this kind of union. There is no reason to remain fixated on a former shade of oneself. *Just get rid of yourself*, Stirner says, and make a new one.

If the state is founded upon prohibiting the un-binding of singularities, the dissolution of unions, and the secession of individuals, then the collapse of the state lies in liberating these activities. To Stirner, this means *insurrection*. In his most infamous passage, Stirner distinguishes between revolution and insurrection, favoring the latter as the proper vehicle of radical ownness:

> Revolution and insurrection must not be looked upon as synonymous. The former consists in an overturning of conditions, of the established condition or status, the state or society, and is accordingly a *political* or *social* act; the latter has indeed for its unavoidable consequence a transformation of circumstances, yet does not start from it but from human beings' discontent with themselves, is not an armed rising, but a rising of individuals, a getting up, without regard to the arrangements that spring from it. The revolution aimed at new *arrangements*; insurrection leads us no longer to *let* ourselves be arranged, but to arrange ourselves, and sets no glittering hopes on 'institutions.' It is not a fight against the established, since, if it prospers, the established collapses of itself; it is only a working forth of me out of the established. If I leave the established, it is dead and passes into decay. Now, as my object is not the overthrow of an established order but my elevation above it, my purpose and deed are not a political or social but (as directed toward myself and my ownness alone) an *egoistic* purpose and deed.[162]

This unarmed rising-up seeks no predetermined arrangements or political institutions except the ones formed by individuals themselves together in struggle. It is the associating of free individuals, the uniting of a union, the expropriating of property—for ourselves, from ourselves. The conditions for revolt may be there already, hidden in the material relations of society, but the deed itself is free, one's own, groundless. It follows the dynamic of self-activity—as Stirner described the goal of *true, free* education. No longer letting ourselves be arranged means taking responsibility for our submission, and acting against it, with or without others, not because of some cause or principle, but from our own discontent. Not in the name of humanity, justice, or freedom, but in the name of nothing. For Stirner, insurrection cannot be limited to an event *in* time. It rather germinates in the uniqueness and ownness of an individual life, and breaks the monotony *of* time. When insurrection takes place at the social level of union or intercourse, only the scale of individuality shifts. But from the perspective of the unique, scale is irrelevant; the individual—as I *or* we—can always revolt. There is no need to wait for an event, the insurrection can begin.

Notes

1. EO, 290
2. EO, 135
3. EO, 163–4
4. Stirner distances himself explicitly from Fichte at EO 163, 267, 318. Although Stirner's finite I and Fichte's transcendental I are incompatible, Fichte also has a separate account of the practical, finite I. It can be found in his *Foundations of Natural Right* of 1796/7. Fichte's argument is based on a *transcendental deduction* of the concept of *right* for a rational free being. It would thus also be roundly rejected by Stirner.
5. This case was convincingly made by Lawrence S. Stepelevich in his article, "Max Stirner as Hegelian" (1985). See page 605. For a contrary view, see De Ridder (2008).
6. For more on Absolute Knowing in Hegel, see Blumenfeld, "The Abolition of Time in Hegel's *Absolute Knowing* (and its relation to Marx)," *Idealistic Studies*, 2014.
7. Hegel, *Phenomenology* (1977), §799. Translation modified.
8. Stepelevich (1985), 606–7
9. EO, 66
10. Deleuze, *Nietzsche and Philosophy*, 159

11. EO, 162

12. EO, 124

13. EO, 275

14. See EO, 11, Stirner's epigraph to Part One of *Der Einzige*: "'Man is to man the supreme being', says Feuerbach. 'Man has just been discovered,' says Bruno Bauer. Then let us take a more careful look at this supreme being and this new discovery."

15. EO, 164

16. EO, 201

17. EO, 192

18. EO, 133

19. For instance, see Strawson, *Individuals* (1959).

20. Hobbes, *Leviathan* (1994), Part I, Chapter IV, "Of Speech," 17

21. Locke, *An Essay Concerning Human Understanding* (1975), Book III, Chapter III, "Of general terms," 409

22. Borges, *Collected Fictions* (1998), 137. Trans modified.

23. Leibniz (1969), 128

24. Spinoza, *Ethics* (1994), part I, proposition 8, scholium II, 89; part I, proposition 10, scholium, 91

25. *Ibid.*, part I, proposition 15, scholium IV, 96

26. *Ibid.*, part II, definition 7, 116

27. EO, 58

28. EO, 156

29. EO, 227. Stirner uses both the German words *Gewalt* and *Macht*, which have a range of meanings not conveyed by the English language. *Gewalt* can be power, force, violence, or even authority; *Macht* can be power, might, rule, strength.

30. EO, 228

31. EO, 227

32. EO, 166

33. EO, 187

34. See Jensen (2006), Brobjer (2003).

35. Many of the first critical writings on Nietzsche in the early 20th century dealt with Stirner side by side. For example, see Albert Lévy, *Stirner et Nietzsche* (1904).

36. Nietzsche, *On the Advantage and Disadvantage of History for Life* (1980), 55

37. EO, 283

38. Nietzsche (1980), 64

39. See Nietzsche, *The Will to Power* (1968), Book Three, Part III, Chapter 2: "The Individual."

40. *Ibid.*, 200 (#373)

41. *Ibid.*, 403 (#767)

42. *Ibid.*, 403 (#768)

43. See Acosta, "How the Stirner Eats Gods" (2009).

44. Nietzsche (1968), 199 (#370)

45. *Ibid.*, 411–412 (#784)

46. Proudhon, *What is Property?* (1970), 42

47. *Ibid.*, 43

48. EO, 223

49. *Ibid.* This sentence is preceded by the following: "Proudhon (Weitling too) thinks he is telling the worst about property when he calls it theft (*vol*). Completely ignoring the embarrassing question of what well-founded objection could be made against theft, we only ask: Is the concept 'theft' at all possible unless one allows validity to the concept of 'property'? How can one steal if property does not already exist? What belongs to no one cannot be *stolen*; one *does not steal* the water that is drawn from the sea."

50. EO, 222

51. *Ibid.*

52. To be fair, Proudhon, does not only say "property is theft." He makes several other arguments concerning the antinomies of property. Without going into it, the core paradoxes can be written as such: property is theft, property is freedom, property is necessary, property is impossible.

See *Property is Theft! A Pierre-Joseph Proudhon Anthology,* ed. McKay (2011).

53. EO, 224

54. EO, 245. For more on the logic of occupation, see Blumenfeld, "Occupation and Revolution" in: Blumenfeld, Bottici, and Critchley, *The Anarchist Turn* (2013), 235–245.

55. Property can be taken by another only if it is *rivalrous,* meaning that one person's use of it is mutually exclusive with someone else's use of it. *Nonrivalrous* property, on the other hand, has no such scarce quality, and can be shared equally by all. An example of rivalrous property is food, whereas an example of nonrivalrous property is radio frequency. If I eat an apple, you cannot eat the same one I just ate; but if you are listening to a radio station, I can listen to the same one without a problem. Stirner does not explicitly mention this distinction, but he accounts for it later with his theory of the "union of *Is*", in which all can benefit from the same property without diminishing it.

56. EO, 128

57. For the classic analysis of fixation as a pathology of ego development, see Freud, *Three Essays on the Theory of Sexuality* (2000). Freud's concept of "Besetzung", which is etymologically close to Stirner's own terminology of possession and occupation, was iconically translated with the neologism "cathexis" by James Strachey. Freud, in fact, was influenced by Eduard von Hartmann's classic work of 1869 entitled *Philosophy of the Unconscious,* which had nine editions by 1882 (and, as already noted, was important for Nietzsche's own development). In that book, von Hartmann wrote that Stirner's *Der Einzige und sein Eigentum* is a book that no one interested in practical philosophy should leave unread. See Hartmann (1931).

58. On the destruction of property as proof of ownership, see Kaspar, "We Demand Nothing" (2009). See also Stirner's

defense of vandalism: "Is the vandal who destroys artworks for which he feels nothing more egoistic than the art connoisseur who treats the same works with great love and care because he has a feeling and interest for them?" *Stirner's Critics* (2012), 81

59. EO, 305–306

60. EO, 143

61. For a contemporary critique of identity, alienation and the "self" along lines similar to Stirner, see the writings of the Invisible Committee, such as *The Coming Insurrection* (2009), *To Our Friends* (2014) and *Now* (2017).

62. See Sartre, *Being and Nothingness* (1992), as well as his early work, *The Transcendence of the Ego* (1957).

63. EO, 154

64. Hegel, *Encyclopedia Logic* (1991), §96 addition

65. EO, 147

66. EO, 210

67. Heidegger, *Being and Time* (1996),§9

68. *Ibid.*, §9

69. *Ibid.*

70. For a critique of authenticity in Heidegger, see Critchley, "Originary Inauthenticity" in: Critchley and Schürmann, *On Heidegger's Being and Time* (2008), 132–151. For a more unsympathetic critique, see Adorno, *The Jargon of Authenticity* (2003).

71. Foucault, *Hermeneutics of the Subject* (2005), 251

72. See Epictetus, *The Handbook* (*Enchiridion*), 11.

73. Foucault (2005), 252

74. EO, 148

75. *Ibid.*

76. *Ibid.*

77. EO, 151. Emphasis mine.

78. EO, 145

79. Stirner uses "grace" to describe the *unowned* relation

between a spook and I. For example, "Right is above me, absolute, and exists in a higher being, as its grace flows to me: right is a gift of grace from the judge; power and might exist only in me, the powerful and mighty." EO, 187

80. Mackay, 127
81. EO, 251
82. *Ibid.*
83. *Ibid.*
84. EO, 104. The following uncited quotes are all from this page.
85. EO, 105
86. *Ibid.*
87. EO, 152
88. EO, 163
89. EO, 135
90. Derrida in: Borradori, *Philosophy in a Time of Terror* (2003), 94
91. EO, 324
92. EO, 185
93. *Ibid.*
94. EO, 300
95. EO, 7
96. EO, 294
97. See *Stirner's Critics* (2012), 58: "Only when nothing is said about you and you are merely named, are you recognized as you. As soon as something is said about you, you are only recognized as that thing (human, spirit, Christian, etc.). But the unique doesn't say anything because it is merely a name: it says only that you are you and nothing but you, that you are a unique you, or rather your self. Therefore, you have no attribute, but with this you are at the same time without determination, vocation, laws, etc."
98. *Ibid.*, 54, 57
99. *Ibid.*, 57

100. EO, 186
101. Levinas, Totality and Infinity (1969), 175. Final italics mine.
102. *Ibid.*, 118
103. EO, 151
104. For more on Levinas and egoism, see Blumenfeld, "Egoism, Labour, and Possession." *The Journal of the British Society for Phenomenology*, Vol. 45, No. 2 (2014).
105. EO, 283
106. EO, 284
107. EO, 179
108. EO, 81
109. EO, 209
110. Marx and Engels, *The German Ideology*, MECW 5: 137
111. Derrida, *Specters of Marx* (1994), 132
112. EO 55, 204
113. EO, 145
114. EO, 179
115. EO, 198
116. EO, 299
117. EO, 209
118. EO, 312
119. EO, 312–313
120. See Bernd A. Laska, "Max Stirner, a durable dissident," for instance.
121. Landauer, "Anarchic Thoughts on Anarchism" in: Landauer, *Revolution and Other Writings* (2010), 84–91
122. *Ibid.*, 85
123. *Ibid.*
124. *Ibid.*, 87
125. *Ibid.*
126. *Ibid.*
127. *Ibid.*, 88
128. Scholem (1965), 112–3. See also Dan (2006), 75; Schwartz (2004), 122–124.

129. See Scholem, 116–7: "But to bring about the *tikkun* and the corresponding state of the cosmos is precisely the aim of redemption. In redemption, everything is restored to its place by the secret magic of human acts, things are freed from their mixture and consequently, in the realms both of man and of nature, from their servitude to the demonic powers, which, once the light is removed from them, are reduced to deathly passivity. In a sense, the tikkun is not so much a restoration of Creation — which though planned was never fully carried out — as its first complete fulfillment."

130. *Ibid.*, 117

131. On "mystical anarchism", see Critchley, *Faith of the Faithless* (2012).

132. EO, 209

133. Landauer, 88–89. Italics mine.

134. *Ibid.*, 89

135. EO, 263

136. EO, 313

137. Landauer, 90. For a similar understanding of anarchy and communism, see Invisible Committee, "Spread anarchy, live communism" in Blumenfeld, Bottici, and Critchley, *The Anarchist Turn* (2013), 224–234.

138. See EO, 316.

139. See EO, 160–1: "If the state is a *society of human beings*, not a *Union of Is*, each of whom has only himself before his eyes, then it cannot last without morality, and must insist on morality."

140. EO, 160

141. See Marx, MECW 28: 23, 132; MECW 29: 91–92, 94, 133, 210, 465, 468.

142. EO, 161

143. On Hegel's concept of "being with oneself in another", see Wood, *Hegel's Ethical Thought* (1990), 45–51; Neuhouser, *Foundations of Hegel's Social Theory* (2000), 19–25.

144. Hegel, *Elements of the Philosophy of Right* (1991), §23
145. EO, 273
146. On the critique of politics, see Invisible Committee, *Now* (2017), 51–89; "Spread anarchy, live communism" in Blumenfeld, Bottici, Critchley (ed.) *The Anarchist Turn* (2013), 224–234.
147. Debord, *Society of the Spectacle* (1995), §1
148. *Ibid.*, §25, §32, §3, §215. It should be noted that the spectacle for Debord is not just a form of generalized separation, but of *unity-in-separation*. "The phenomenon of separation is part and parcel of the unity of the world" (§7). Spectacle thus encompasses the "social organization of appearances" (§10), the integration of society through its disintegration. Thanks to EJ Russell for the tips here.
149. On Debord's Hegelian-Marxism and his debt to Lukács, see Jappe (1999), Russell (2015), Bunyard (2018).
150. Debord (1995), §24
151. EO, 271
152. *Ibid.*
153. EO, 276. Italics mine.
154. Spinoza, *Ethics* (1994),126. Italics mine.
155. Stirner, "The False Principle of Our Education" (1842). The form of *freedom* which Stirner lauds here is self-emancipation, not negative freedom. It is thus closer to what he will eventually call *ownness*.
156. *Ibid.*
157. EO, 61
158. EO, 192
159. Agamben, *The Coming Community* (1993), 86
160. Badiou, *Being and Event* (2005), 109
161. Agamben, 86
162. EO, 279

All Things are Nothing to Me: Stirner, Marx and Communism

Why still read Max Stirner today?

Because now that we live at the end of history, it might do us some good to look at a few of the first ideas that pointed beyond it. In the 1840s, Germany was teeming with philosophical critiques of bourgeois society, while France was burgeoning with practical revolts against it. It was Stirner's genius to attack the left Hegelian critics of religion, politics and society for remaining trapped within the liberal ideology of their day, and for basing their political positions on nothing more than secularized Christian values, separate from any relation to the material concerns of individuals. And it was Marx's brilliance to embed Stirner's critique of ideology within a historical analysis of class antagonisms and social relations of production.

It is commonplace that Marx developed the materialist conception of history in *The German Ideology* around 1845. But how did he do so? Although Marx already had a sophisticated philosophical account of alienation and private property, it was not until he responded to Stirner's 1844 *Der Einzige und sein Eigentum* that his philosophical-political critique became thoroughly historical. If reading Stirner gave Marx and Engels the impetus for a historical materialist critique, then what else can it give us today? Is there a way to read Stirner with fresh eyes, as Engels first did when he wrote to Marx after reading it that, "clearly Stirner is the most talented, independent and hard-working of the 'Free', but for all that he tumbles out of idealistic into materialistic abstraction and ends up in limbo."[1]

What is this limbo into which Stirner falls? It is surely the ambiguous zone between idealism and materialism, between the heaven of thought and hell of labor. Stirner may have escaped the idealist presuppositions of Hegelian philosophy, according to Engels, but he has not moved beyond idealistic targets. In other words, although Stirner starts with real individuals, he only confronts idealistic phantasms, or in Engels's terms, "materialistic abstractions". Stirner's anti-ideological struggle consists in demystifying abstractions and criticizing fetishes such as God, Man, State, Society, Morality, Justice, Labor, Equality, Freedom, Love, and Revolution. In one of his more spectacular moments, Stirner names his burden as "storming heaven", a task only completed with the "real, complete downfall of heaven."[2] Even Satan was too narrow, for he focused solely on Earth. Stirner eventually called this method *desecration*. Engels again: "This egoism is taken to such a pitch, it is so absurd and at the same time so self-aware, that it cannot maintain itself even for an instant in its one-sidedness, but must immediately change into communism. In the first place, it is a simple matter to prove to Stirner that his egoistic man is bound to become communist out of sheer egoism. That's the way to answer the fellow."[3]

Thus, Marx and Engels responded to Stirner in the massive section of *The German Ideology* called "Saint Max". They do not criticize Stirner's "egoism" for being the opposite of communism, as many people think, but rather they show that egoism must immediately "change into communism", that "egoistic man" is bound to become "communist" out of egoism alone. But not only this. Engels admits that, "we must also adopt such truth as there is in the principle. And it is certainly true that we must first make a cause our own, egoistic cause, before we can do anything to further it—and hence that in this sense, irrespective of any eventual material aspirations, we are communists out of egoism also."[4] Not only does egoism lead to communism, but egoism is the *first cause of* communism, its ground and foundation, that which motivates individuals to become communists before anything else. Engels emphasizes this to Marx: "*We must take our departure from the I, the empirical, flesh-and-blood individual.*"[5] Perhaps the following passage from Stirner convinced Engels to begin with the needs of the individual, instead of some cause outside it:

> People have always supposed that they must give me a destiny lying outside myself, so that at last they demanded that I should lay claim to the human because I am—human. This is the Christian magic circle. Fichte's I too is the same essence outside me, for everyone is I; and, if only this I has rights, then it is 'the I', I am not it. But I am not an I along with other Is, but the sole I: I am unique. Hence my needs too are unique, and my actions; in short, everything about me is unique. And it is only as this unique I that I take everything for my own, as I set myself to work, and develop myself, only as this. I do not develop human beings, nor as a human being, but, as I, I develop—myself. This is the meaning of the—*unique one* [*Einzigen*].[6]

Reading Stirner caused Engels to rethink the primary motivation for communism, "the real movement which abolishes the present state of things."[7] No communist movement can ever succeed unless it's rooted in the base egoism of individuals seeking a better life for themselves. In other words, if the first cause of communism is *myself*, the will to better my own conditions and live without alienation, exploitation, and dead time, then out of this sheer egoism alone, I will be forced to become a communist. For how else will I transform my own individual situation of misery without confronting the social conditions that produce it? Hence, in order to become "the unique" agent of our own lives that Stirner demands, we must unite with others to abolish the conditions that constrain us. For Stirner, these self-produced yet alien conditions rule our conceptual and material existence; both forms of domination must be attacked. For Marx and Engels, however, while it is essential to challenge the ideological mystifications of our suffering, the unfreedom of our daily lives will only end with the end of the specific economic system that reproduces it.

Engels and Marx were not the first to point out that Stirner's egoist must also be communist. Feuerbach made this same claim in his 1845 reply to Stirner: "To be an individual is certainly, of course, to be an 'Egoist,' but it is also at the same time and indeed unintentionally to be a 'communist.'"[8] Feuerbach did not mean this politically, however, but philosophically, insofar as any I is only an I in relation to others. This is a simple Hegelian point, and Stirner himself agrees. In his reply to Feuerbach, he notes that "it does not occur to him [Stirner] to deny that the 'individual' is 'communist.'"[9] Any individual, to Stirner, is of course social, communal, relational; it is all those things — and *more*. The unique participates fully in life, with others, freely and joyfully, and yet it is not exhausted by its relations with others. What the unique excludes in its exclusivity is only aliety, fixity, sacredness, disinterestedness, the uninteresting.[10] An anti-social, narcissistic I is possible, but pathetic, for "this would be someone who does not know and relish all the joys that come from participation with others, i.e., from thinking of others as well, someone who lacks countless pleasures — thus a poor sort."[11]

Stirner not only provoked quite the spirited response in his contemporaries, but also long after. His influence can be seen in Friedrich Nietzsche, Emma Goldman, Dora Marsden, Jules Bonnot, Renzo Novatore, Carl Schmitt, Edmund Husserl, Gustav Landauer, Wilhelm Reich, Victor Serge, Marcel Duchamp, Herbert Marcuse, Albert Camus and Raoul Vaneigem. If nothing else, reading Stirner has historically proven time and again to reawaken the spirit of revolt that animates the radical critique of everyday life. This revolt is not grounded in some external social cause or political ideal, but first of all in the relationship to one's own life.

Another reason to read Stirner today is to see the parallels and problems in certain tendencies of contemporary critical thought. The movement from left-Hegelians through Stirner to Marx could shed some light on the dynamic of left-wing critique today. The young Hegelians, the "Free", criticized bourgeois society for not living up to its ideal of *humanity*, of failing to bring justice, equality, and freedom to all who live within the modern state. They criticized governments, advocated for "social justice", wrote in newspapers and signed petitions. Are they not the cell-form of the modern activist today, the social justice warrior who endlessly searches for the latest ideal to foreground the hypocrisy of bad individuals and states? Both advocate for "people power", for self-managed "free states", for the triumph of a secular humanity against the backwardness of religion. Against this, Stirner attacks the normative foundations upon which such critiques stand, that is, ideas of mankind, law, justice, equality, society and freedom. He claims that these criteria are nothing but reified abstractions of alienated relations which obfuscate one's own condition. In effect, they turn the ideal itself into the foundation of the real.

Stirner's anti-moral, anti-state, and anti-work critique ends up defending *insurrection* against revolution, for whereas "the revolution aimed at new *arrangements*; insurrection leads us no longer to *let* ourselves be arranged."[12] Perhaps this is the original template for the contemporary radical critique of liberal activism. Stirner's heirs cut through the abstractions that litter the field of possibilities for the future, spooks such as "participatory economics", "social justice", "democratic socialism", or "self-management." Stirner sees no hope outside the negation of the present, the consumption of all things into nothing for me, the dissolution and reabsorption of everything separate from individuals. Only by patiently attending to each particular abstraction and pulling at its roots can something like another future be possible. For Stirner, the roots of our abstract domination lie in our false idols of god and state, hierarchy and government, work and society. In a quite Stirnerist moment, Marx claims that if anything remains separate from individuals, then alienation has not been overcome, and communism is still not achieved:

> Communism differs from all previous movements in that it overturns the basis of all earlier relations of production and intercourse, and for the first time consciously treats all natural premises as the creatures of hitherto existing human beings, strips them of their natural character and subjugates them to the power of the *united individuals*. Its organisation is, therefore, essentially economic, the material production of the conditions of this unity; it turns existing conditions into conditions of unity. *The reality, which communism is creating, is precisely the true basis for rendering it impossible that anything should exist independently of individuals, insofar as reality is only a product of the preceding intercourse of individuals themselves.*[13]

Under the power of "united individuals", communism creates a reality in which nothing should "exist independently of individuals". Communism for Marx is thus not so different from egoism for Stirner, since both seek to wrest control of individual life from domination by real abstractions. For Marx, these abstractions are rooted in the economic relations of production, and hence should be strategically confronted in that sphere. For Stirner, they are everywhere, and so can be attacked anywhere one finds them.

Marx thus did not ignore Stirner's intervention and return to the framework of the young Hegelians. Rather, he sought to materially ground the source of the abstractions that Stirner criticizes. One by one, Marx located the material social relations that gave birth to the dominant ideologies of the day. Stirner traces modern liberal ideas back to their reliance on some alienated concept of god, state, or humanity, and then utterly desecrates it, advocating for crime, the inhuman, secession. Marx, on the other hand, situates Stirner's critique of abstract domination within the orbit of private property, capital, and class struggle. Equality, property, freedom and justice for Marx are all historically specific conceptions that emerge from the material relations amongst human beings in capitalist society. To Marx, these ideal abstractions reflect the real abstraction of capital, the objective form of alienated human activity generated in modern societies based on the production of commodities for exchange. According to Marx, the historical dynamic of capital subsumes the content of human activity under the specific form of labor directed towards value, in turn inverting the subject and object of history.[14] Albeit confusedly, Stirner grasped the abstract form of domination that inverts subjective agency in capitalist society, and he sought to reappropriate it for himself. He wanted to break with the objective and subjective mediations of bourgeois society, everything that reduces individuals to social functions, perceptible attributes, or normative values. However, it can be argued that Stirner conflated the *form* of abstract domination with its *content*. Nevertheless, Stirner was the first and most radical author to pose the problem of how an individual can break with the totalizing social synthesis of modernity.

In *The German Ideology*, Marx paints Stirner as a modern Don Quixote and a new Saint Paul, a knight errant and militant apostle against the old gods. Saint Max, or Sancho, as Marx trolled him, failed to target the historically specific material relations that animate our modern gods. One way of understanding Marx's critique is to say that Stirner's unique individual, the *Einzige* or *I* capable of fully developing its own powers, is only possible in fully developed communism, the state of affairs in which material relations are inseparable from individual power and not dependent on the drive for valorization. In a formula, *Stirner's egoism is Marx's communism seen from the first person singular perspective.* It is not the negation but the realization of the individual. Chasing Stirner throughout *The German Ideology*, Marx echoes him when writing the following description of communism as the free development of *individuals*:

We have already shown above that the abolition of a state of affairs in which relations become independent of *individuals*, in which *individuality* is subservient to chance and the personal relations of *individuals* are subordinated to general class relations, etc.—that the abolition of this state of affairs is determined in the final analysis by the abolition of division of labour… Within communist society, the only society in which the genuine and free development of *individuals* ceases to be a mere phrase, this development is determined precisely by the connection of *individuals*, a connection which consists partly in the economic prerequisites and partly in the necessary solidarity of the free development of all, and, finally, in the universal character of the activity of *individuals* on the basis of the existing productive forces.[15]

Communism is the society of free individuals—Marx understood this, and so did many readers of Stirner. In Emma Goldman's *Mother Earth* magazine from 1907, the German-American anarchist Max Baginski wrote the following review of the first English translation of *Der Einzige und sein Eigentum*: "Communism thus creates a basis for the liberty and *Eigenheit* of the individual. I am a Communist *because* I am an Individualist. Fully as heartily the Communists concur with Stirner when he puts the word *take* in place of *demand*—that leads to the dissolution of property, to expropriation. Individualism and Communism go hand in hand."[16] In 1974, the American situationist collective *For Ourselves* published "The Right to Be Greedy: Theses on the Practical Necessity of Demanding Everything," a pamphlet affirming the radical synthesis of Marx and Stirner, of communism and egoism:

'Communist egoism' names the synthesis of individualism and collectivism, just as communist society names the actual, material, sensuous solution to the historical contradiction of the 'particular' and the 'general' interest, a contradiction engendered especially in the cleavage of society against itself into classes. This 'solution' cannot be of the form of a mere idea or abstraction, but only of a concrete form of society… The essence of communism is egoism; the essence of egoism is communism. This is the world-changing secret which the world at large still keeps from itself. The unraveling of this secret as the emergence of radical subjectivity is nothing other than the process of the formation of communist society itself. It already contains the objective process.[17]

Sadly, but unsurprisingly, the "secret" of communist egoism has not been taken up since—neither by communists nor individualists, Marxists nor anarchists.

Marx, however, did more than just ground the possibility of Stirner's individualism in the condition of communism. He ties Stirner's theoretical criticisms of bourgeois society to the practical, proletarian struggles already occurring in Western Europe. For Marx, criticism does not need to *represent* such struggles, but rather only *express* their object in the fullest possible way. This object or target, for which Stirner clears the ground, is capital, and the proletarian insurrections of the 1840s are implicitly if not explicitly against it. Is there a Marx of today, a critic that can situate the critical response to the left in a global field of antagonism against the target of capital? Perhaps this is the need: to connect proletarian revolt to its object in a manner which explains the dynamics of capital and self, property and its negation.

That said, I can now return to Stirner one last time, from the beginning. First, through an analysis of the borrowed line with which he starts and ends his book, and second, with some final thoughts on the unique, the proletariat, and the creative nothing.

Ich hab' Mein Sach' auf Nichts gestellt. All things are nothing to me. I have set my affair on nothing. I place my trust in nothing.

—That is how it begins, and follows,

> What is not supposed to be my concern! First and foremost, the good cause, then God's cause, the cause of mankind, of truth, of freedom, of humanity, of justice; further, the cause of my people, my prince, my fatherland; finally, even the cause of mind, and a thousand other causes. Only my cause is never to be my concern. *Shame on the egoist who thinks only of himself!*[18]

Stirner steals his opening line from a nihilistic, drinking song-poem from 1806 by Goethe called "Vanitas! Vanitatum Vanitas!" It goes like this:

> My trust in nothing now is placed [*All things are nothing to me*]
> > Hurrah!
> So in the world true joy I taste,
> > Hurrah!
> Then he who would be a comrade of mine
> Must rattle his glass, and in chorus combine,
> Over these dregs of wine.
>
> I placed my trust in gold and wealth,
> Hurrah!
> But then I lost all joy and health,
> > Ah, ha!
> Both here and there the money roll'd,
> And when I had it here, behold,
> From there had fled the gold!
>
> I placed my trust in women next,
> > Hurrah!
> But there in truth was sorely vex'd,
> > Ah, ha!

The False another portion sought,
The True with tediousness were fraught,
The Best could not be bought.

My trust in travels then I placed,
	Hurrah!
And left my native land in haste.
	Ah, ha!
But not a single thing seem'd good,
The beds were bad, and strange the food,
And I not understood.

I placed my trust in rank and fame,
	Hurrah!
Another put me straight to shame,
	Ah, ha!
And as I had been prominent,
All scowl'd upon me as I went,
I found not one content.

I placed my trust in war and fight,
	Hurrah!
We gain'd full many a triumph bright,
	Hurrah!
Into the foeman's land we cross'd,
We put our friends to equal cost,
And there a leg I lost.

My trust is placed in nothing now, [*All things are nothing to me*]
	Hurrah!
At my command the world must bow,
	Hurrah!
And as we've ended feast and strain,

The cup we'll to the bottom drain;
No dregs must there remain![19]

As with Stirner, Goethe deals with the hopelessness of searching for causes outside oneself. Consuming life in numerous activities such as money, sex, travels, fame, and war, the individual nevertheless fails to identify with any of them. Everything is nothing to them. The protagonist of Goethe's poem invests various objects, activities and relationships with its own ideal of who it wants to be, and is repeatedly disappointed. Liberation and joy ultimately comes from breaking the inner compulsion to identify with anything at all, and instead, treating the world like property to be consumed in enjoyment with others. For Stirner, Goethe describes the wandering subject of the present, the I without qualities who can only become unique by appropriating their emptiness and using it as fuel for life.

The title of the poem, "Vanitas! Vanitatum Vanitas!", comes from Ecclesiastes chapter 1 verse 2, which Jerome's Latin renders as *Vanitas vanitatum dixit Ecclesiastes vanitas vanitatum omnia vanitas*. A modern translation reads, "Vanity of vanities, said the Preacher: vanity of vanities, all is vanity." Vanity here signifies a certain emptiness or meaninglessness, the transitory impermanence of all labor or activity under the sun, under God. The original Hebrew word for vanitas is *Hevel*, which means breath, or sometimes fog. *Hevel* is also the name of the first son in the Bible, Abel, the first worker, whose short life of labor is as meaningless as modern life under capital. However, in between the Hebrew and Latin, the Greek Septuagint translated Hevel as *mataiotes*, "devoid of truth, useless" which comes from the verb *masaomai*, which means "to chew, eat, devour."

This is especially interesting, since Stirner's main concept of action is *consumption*, by which he means the taking, seizing, and releasing of things from their sacred sphere to the sphere of *free use* and *abuse*. To consume is to use, and if the world is *vanity*, *hevel, masomai,* that is, empty, useless, already chewed up, then the task is not to refill it with new abstractions, but to consume it anew, to masticate it ourselves. The world as we know it is dead, consumed labor, it is *nothing to me.* But this nothing is not a general or empty nothing, it is the particular nothing of capital which confronts the particular nothing of I. These two nothings are *distinct*: "I am not nothing in the sense of emptiness, but I am the creative nothing, the nothing out of which I myself as creator create everything."[20] This creative nothing does not escape the nihilism of capital by retreating into qualities, identities, or properties. Only by expropriating what expropriates me, by making the world into *my* property, is something like communist egoism possible.

To Stirner, there is really no difference between saying "the world belongs to everyone" and "the world belongs to me." Communism and egoism are compatible as long as "everyone" is not reified into a new ruling subject above me, as Stirner notes:

What the human being can get belongs to him: the world belongs to *me.* Are you saying anything else with the opposite proposition: 'The world belongs to *all*'? All are I and I again, etc. But you make a spook out of the 'all' and make it sacred, so that the 'all' become the fearful *master* of the individual. Then the ghost of 'right' stands at their side.[21]

To make the world one's property cannot occur without the dissolution of the bourgeois state and civil society, and replacing it with communes, associations, unions, and councils. "The dissolution of society is intercourse or union," but such unions are not guaranteed to last, especially if their form predetermines their content. "If a union has crystallized into a society...if it has become a unitedness, come to a standstill, degenerated into a fixity; it is—*dead* as union, it is the corpse of the union or unification, it is—society, community."[22]

When society or community becomes the privileged form of the individual's self-relation, then the task of the unique is to desecrate society as much as possible. Capital desecrates history, wastes human labor and squanders the planet. But Stirner's unique does not retreat in the face of this power, petitioning for some penance. Rather, the free association of individuals desecrates capital, wastes its value, and owns the future. The subject produced through such activity is not some kind of Nietzschean *Übermensch*, but what Stirner calls an *Unmensch* or *un-man*, one who no longer allows themselves to be classified, exploited, or owned.

In *Capital*, Marx describes the process by which things take on social relations (the personification of things) and persons take on thingly relations (the reification of persons). Stirner's "all things are nothing to me" condenses this dual-process all the while pronouncing a strategy beyond it as well. His lesson: one must follow the path of alienation towards its overcoming. To annihilate the world is the purpose of *both* capital, which negates the content of human activity and replaces it with the form-determined imperatives of value, *and* communism, which annuls the thinglike quality of the world, and allows free individuals to use, consume and dissolve each other in union. "All that is solid melts into air, all that is holy is profaned"—this is the power of capital as Marx and Engels describe it in the *Communist Manifesto*. For Marx *and* Stirner, this power to dissolve all "fixed, fast-frozen relations" should not be the exclusive property of the bourgeoisie, but mine and yours as well. Once expropriated from its owners, our disalienated social power can dissolve the present state of things. For Marx, there is only one class of society positioned to do this. "This dissolution of society," Marx writes, "is the proletariat," and "by proclaiming the *dissolution of the hitherto existing world order*, the proletariat merely states the *secret of its own existence*, for it is in fact the dissolution of that world order."[23]

As noted before, Deleuze praises Stirner for being the "dialectician who reveals nihilism as the truth of the dialectic."[24] For Deleuze, Stirner demonstrates that "the meaning of history and the dialectic together is not the realization of reason, freedom, or man as species, but nihilism, nothing but nihilism." If the dialectic, however, is more properly understood as the correlate structure of the systematic logic of capital (which Marx outlines in the *Grundrisse* and *Capital*), then what Stirner reveals for Marx is the nothingness of capital, its own particular nihilism. Stirner describes the nothingness of the I as the condition of possibility for becoming unique. From a Marxian perspective, however, this can be read as a description of the nothingness of capital or the negativity of the proletariat—the class which has no particular qualities, but only the generic form of labor power.

To make sense of this ambiguity of perspective, we can take a hint from the structure of Hegel's *Phenomenology of Spirit* and from Marx's *Capital*. In Hegel's *Phenomenology*, the movement of spirit can be seen from the perspective of substance or the perspective of subject, and the "we" of the text is nothing but the mutual constitution of the two. In Marx's *Capital*, the structure of capitalism is seen from both the perspective of capital and labor, and capitalism is nothing but the mutually constitutive relation of the two. For Stirner, the movement of negation occurs between the *unique* and its *properties*, or the *ego* and its *own*. Communism or egoism is not the privileging of one side over the other, but the abolition of the separation between the two from within the negative potential of one. Hegel's subject negates and realizes substance, Stirner's unique negates and realizes property, Marx's proletariat negates and realizes capital.

Stirner struggles to express in words the uniqueness of my nothingness, my singularity. This nothingness is not to be taken "in the sense of emptiness," but rather in the sense of *that from which and into which creation creates*; but that which creates is— *labor*. The unique and the proletariat are both creative nothings, productive yet alienated from themselves, seeking to own and consume that which owns and consumes them.

As nothing, I stand apart, singular. But as a proletarian, my unique nothingness is united with others who, like me, have nothing but want everything. The uniqueness of the proletariat lies in its being the universal negation of society. As Marx says, it is the only class which can defiantly proclaim, in unison with Stirner,

I am nothing and I should be everything.[25]

Notes

1. Engels (1982), 13
2. EO, 65
3. Engels (1982), 12
4. *Ibid*.
5. *Ibid*.
6. EO, 318–9
7. Marx and Engels, *The German Ideology*, MECW 5: 49
8. Feuerbach (1977), 85
9. *Stirner's Critics* (2012), 88
10. See *Stirner's Critics*, 81–2: "Egoism... is not opposed to love nor to thought; it is no enemy of the sweet life of love, nor of devotion and sacrifice; it is no enemy of intimate warmth, but it is also no enemy of critique, nor of socialism, nor, in short, of any *actual interest*. It does not exclude any interest. It is directed against only disinterestedness and the uninteresting; not against love, but against sacred love, not against thought, but against sacred thought, not against socialists, but against sacred socialists, etc. The 'exclusiveness' of the egoist, which some want to pass off as isolation, separation, loneliness, is on the contrary full *participation* in the interesting by—exclusion of the uninteresting. No one gives Stirner credit for his global

intercourse and his association of egoists from the largest section of his book, 'My Intercourse.'"

11. *Ibid.*, 80
12. EO, 279
13. Marx and Engels, *The German Ideology*, MECW 5: 81. Italics mine.
14. For more on this reading of Marx, see Postone (1993).
15. Marx and Engels, *The German Ideology*, MECW 5: 438, 439. Emphasis mine.
16. *Mother Earth*, Vol. 2. No. 3. May, 1907 [Accessed: November 24, 2017]: https://theanarchistlibrary.org/library/max-bagin skistirner-the-ego-and-his-own
17. For Ourselves, *The Right to Be Greedy* (1974), Theses 45, 47
18. EO, 5
19. Translation taken from here [Accessed: November 24, 2017]: https://en.wikisource.org/wiki/The_Works_of_J._W._von_ Goethe/Volume_9/Vanitas,_Vanitatum_Vanitas
20. EO, 7
21. EO, 222
22. EO, 271
23. Marx, MECW 3: 186, 187
24. For this and the following quote, see Deleuze, 161.
25. *"Ich bin nichts, und ich müsste alles sein."* Marx, MECW 3: 185

Bibliography

Primary

Stirner, Max. *The Ego and Its Own* [EO], ed. David Leopold. Cambridge: Cambridge University Press, 1995

-------- *Der Einzige und sein Eigentum*. Germany: Reclam, 2003

-------- *Parerga, Kritiken, Repliken*, ed. Bernd Laska. Germany: LSR-Verlag, 1986

-------- *Stirner's Critics*, tr. Landstreicher. Berkeley: LBC Books, 2012

-------- *The Unique and Its Property*, tr. Landstreicher. Berkeley: Ardent Press, 2018

-------- "The False Principle of Our Education" (1842). [Accessed: November 24, 2017] https://theanarchistlibrary.org/library/maxstirner-the-false-principle-of-our-education

Secondary

Acosta, Alejandro de. "How the Stirner Eats Gods." *Anarchy: A Journal of Desire Armed*, Vol. 26, No. 2, #67, 2009, pp. 28–39

Adorno, Theodor. *Negative Dialectics*. New York: Continuum, 1973

-------- *The Jargon of Authenticity*. London: Routledge, 2003

Agamben, Giorgio. *The Coming Community*, tr. Michael Hardt. Minnesota: University of Minnesota Press, 1993

Arvon, Henri. *Aux Sources de l'existentialisme: Max Stirner*. Paris: Presses Universitaires de France, 1954

Badiou, Alain. *Being and Event*, tr. Oliver Feltham. London: Continuum, 2006

Blumenfeld, Jacob. "The Abolition of Time in Hegel's *Absolute Knowing* (and its relevance for Marx)." *Idealistic Studies*, 2014

-------- "Egoism, Labour, and Possession: A reading of 'Interiority and Economy,' Section II of Lévinas' *Totality and Infinity*." *The Journal of the British Society for Phenomenology*, Vol. 45, No. 2,

107–117, 2014

Blumenfeld, Jacob, Bottici, Chiara and Critchley, Simon (ed.). *The Anarchist Turn*. London: Pluto Press, 2013

Borges, Jorge Luis. *Collected Fictions*, tr. A. Hurley. New York: Viking Penguin, 1998

Borradori, Giovanna. *Philosophy in a Time of Terror*. Chicago: University of Chicago Press, 2003

Brobjer, Thomas H. "Philologica: A Possible Solution to the Stirner-Nietzsche Question." *Journal of Nietzsche Studies*, Issue 25, Spring 2003, pp. 109–114

Buber, Martin. *Between Man and Man*. New York: Routledge, 2002

Bunyard, Tom. *Debord, Time and Spectacle*. Leiden: Brill, 2018

Carroll, John. *Break-Out from the Crystal Palace. The Anarcho-Psychological Critique: Stirner, Nietzsche, Dostoevsky*. London: Routledge and Kegan Paul, 1974

Clark, John P. *Max Stirner's Egoism*. London: Freedom Press, 1976

Critchley, Simon. *Faith of the Faithless*. London: Verso, 2012

Critchley, Simon and Schürmann, Reiner. *On Heidegger's Being and Time*. London: Routledge, 2008

Dan, Joseph. *Kabbalah: A Very Short Introduction*. Oxford: Oxford University Press, 2006

De Ridder, Widukind. "Max Stirner, Hegel, and the Young Hegelians: A reassessment." *History of European Ideas,* 34: 285–297, 2008

Debord, Guy. *The Society of the Spectacle*, tr. Donald Nicholson-Smith. New York: Zone Books, 1995

Deleuze, Gilles. *Nietzsche and Philosophy*, tr. Hugh Tomlinson. New York: Columbia University Press, 1983

Derrida, Jacques. *Specters of Marx*, tr. Peggy Kamuf. New York: Routledge, 1994

Engels, F. "Engels to Karl Marx, 19 November 1844" in *Karl Marx and Frederick Engels Collected Works 38* [MECW 38]. New York: International Publishers, 1982, 9–14

Epictetus. *The Handbook (Enchiridion)*, tr. N. White. Indianapolis:

Hackett, 1983

Essbach, Wolfgang. *Gegenzüge: Der Materialismus des Selbst und seine Ausgrenzung aus dem Marxismus.* Frankfurt am Main: Materialis-Verlag, 1982

Feuerbach, Ludwig. *The Essence of Christianity,* tr. George Elliot. Amherst: Prometheus Books, 1989

-------- "*The Essence of Christianity* in Relation to *The Ego and Its Own,*" tr. F. Gordon. *The Philosophical Forum,* vol. 7, nos. 2–4, (1977), pp. 81–91. [Accessed: November 24, 2017] http://www. lsrprojekt. de/poly/enfeuerbach.html

Fichte, JG. *Foundations of Natural Right,* tr. M. Baur. Cambridge: Cambridge University Press, 2000

For Ourselves. "The Right to Be Greedy: Theses on the Practical Necessity of Demanding Everything" pamphlet. UK, 1974. https://theanarchistlibrary.org/library/for-ourselves-the right-to-be-greedy-theses-on-the-practical-necessity-ofdem anding-everything

Foucault, Michel. *The Hermeneutics of the Subject,* ed. Frederic Gros, tr. Graham Burchell. New York: Picador, 2005

Freud, Sigmund. *Three Essays on the Theory of Sexuality,* tr. J. Strachey. New York: Basic Books, 2000

Hartmann, Eduard Von. *Philosophy of the Unconscious.* New York: Harcourt, 1931

Hegel, GWF. *Science of Logic,* tr. AV Miller. New York: Humanity Books, 1969

-------- *Philosophy of Mind,* tr. W. Wallace. Oxford: Clarendon Press, 1971

-------- *Phenomenology of Spirit,* tr. AV Miller. Oxford: Oxford University Press, 1977

-------- *Introduction to the Philosophy of History,* tr. L. Rauch. Indianapolis: Hackett, 1988

-------- *Encyclopedia Logic,* tr. Geraets, Suchting, and Harris. Indianapolis: Hackett, 1991

-------- *Elements of the Philosophy of Right,* ed. A. Wood. Cambridge:

Cambridge University Press, 1991

Heidegger, Martin. *Being and Time,* tr. Joan Stambaugh. Albany: SUNY Press, 1996

Heider, Ulrike. *Anarchism: Left, Right and Green.* San Francisco: City Lights Books, 1994

Helms, Hans G. *Die Ideology der anonymen.* Cologne: Gesellschaft, 1966

Hobbes, Thomas. Leviathan, ed. E. Curley. Indianapolis: Hackett, 1994

Invisible Committee. *The Coming Insurrection.* Cambridge: Semiotext(e), 2009

-------- *To Our Friends.* Cambridge: Semiotext(e), 2015

-------- *Now.* Cambridge: Semiotext(e), 2017

Jappe, Anselm. *Guy Debord,* tr. Donald Nicholson-Smith. Berkeley: University of California Press, 1999

Jensen, Anthony. "The Rogue of All Rogues: Nietzsche's Presentation of Eduard von Hartmann's 'Philosophie des Unbewussten' and Hartmann's Response to Nietzsche." *Journal of Nietzsche Studies,* Issue 32, Autumn 2006

Kaspar, Johann. "We Demand Nothing" in: Fire to the Prisons (Issue 7), 2009. Online at: https://theanarchistlibrary.org/ library/johann-kaspar-we-demand-nothing

Kast, Bernd. *Max Stirners Destruktion der spekulativen Philosophie.* Freiburg: Verlag Karl Alber, 2016

Koch, Andrew M. "Max Stirner: The Last Hegelian or the First Poststructuralist." *Anarchist Studies,* Volume 5 (1997), pp. 95–107

Landauer, Gustav. *Revolution and Other Writings,* ed. G. Kuhn. Oakland: PM Press, 2010

Lange, F. *The History of Materialism,* tr. Ernest Chester Thomas. New York: Humanities Press, 1950

Laska, Bernd A. "Max Stirner, a durable dissident—in a nutshell." *Die Zeit,* Nr. 5, 27, Seite 49, tr. by Shveta Thakrar, Januar 2000

Leibniz, Gottfried Wilhelm. *Philosophical Papers and Letters.*

Translated by Leroy E. Loemker. 2nd edition. Dordrecht: Kluwer, 1969

Levinas, Emmanuel. *Totality and Infinity*. Pittsburgh: Duquesne University Press, 1969

Lévy, Albert. *Stirner et Nietzsche*. Paris: Societé Nouvelle de Librairie et d'Édition, 1904

Link-Salinger (Hyman), Ruth. *Gustav Landauer: Philosopher of Utopia*. Indianapolis: Hackett, 1977

Locke, John. *An Essay Concerning Human Understanding*. Oxford: Clarendon Press, 1975

Löwith, Karl. *From Hegel to Nietzsche: The Revolution in Nineteenth-Century Thought*. London: Constable, 1965

Mackay, John Henry. *Max Stirner: His Life and His Work*, tr. Hubert Kennedy. Concord: Peremptory Publications, 2005

Marx, Karl. *On the Jewish Question* in *Karl Marx and Frederick Engels Collected Works 3* [MECW 3]. New York: International Publishers, 1975, 146–175

-------- "Contribution to the Critique of Hegel's Philosophy of Law. Introduction" in *Karl Marx and Frederick Engels Collected Works 3* [MECW 3]. New York: International Publishers, 1975, 175–187

-------- "Economic Manuscripts of 1857-58" in *Karl Marx and Frederick Engels Collected Works 28-29* [MECW 28–29]. New York: International Publishers, 1986-87

-------- *Capital: A Critique of Political Economy, Volume One*, in *Karl Marx and Frederick Engels Collected Works 35* [MECW 35]. New York: International Publishers, 1996

Marx, K. and Engels, F. *The German Ideology* in *Karl Marx and Frederick Engels Collected Works 5* [MECW 5]. New York: International Publishers, 1975, 19–585

McKay, Iain. *Property is Theft! A Pierre-Joseph Proudhon Anthology*. Oakland: AK Press, 2011

McLellan, David. *The Young Hegelians and Karl Marx*. London: Palgrave, 1969

Moggach, Douglas. *The New Hegelians*. Cambridge: Cambridge University Press, 2006

Nagle, Angela. *Kill All Normies*. Winchester: Zero Books, 2017

Neuhouser, Frederick. *Foundations of Hegel's Social Theory*. Cambridge: Harvard University Press, 2000

Newman, Saul. *From Bakunin to Lacan*. Plymouth: Lexington Books, 2001

-------- *The Politics of Postanarchism*. Edinburgh: Edinburgh University Press, 2010

-------- (ed.) *Max Stirner*. New York: Palgrave Macmillan, 2011

-------- *Postanarchism*. Cambridge: Polity, 2016

Nietzsche, Friedrich. *On the Advantage and Disadvantage of History for Life*, tr. Peter Preuss. Indianapolis: Hackett, 1980

-------- *The Will to Power*, tr. Walter Kaufmann. New York: Vintage, 1968

Paterson, RWK. *The Nihilistic Egoist Max Stirner*. London: Oxford University Press, 1971

Postone, Moishe. *Time, Labor, and Social Domination: A Reinterpretation of Marx's Critical Theory*. Cambridge: Cambridge University Press, 1993

Proudhon, P-J. *What is Property?* ed. George Woodcock, tr. Benjamin Tucker. New York: Dover Publications, 1970

Russell, Eric-John. Review of Ken Knabb's translation of "Society of the Spectacle." *Marx and Philosophy Review of Books*, 2015. [Accessed: November 24, 2017] https://marxandphilosophy.org.uk/reviewofbooks/reviews/2015/1471

Sartre, Jean-Paul. *The Transcendence of the Ego,* tr. F. Williams and R. Kirkpatrick. New York: Noonday Press, 1957

-------- *Being and Nothingness*. New York: Washington Square Press, 1992

Scholem, Gershom. *On the Kabbalah and Its Symbolism*. New York: Schocken Books, 1965

Schwartz, Howard. *Tree of Souls*. Oxford: Oxford University Press, 2004

Spinoza, Benedict de. "Ethics" in: Curley, Edwin, ed. *A Spinoza Reader*. Princeton: Princeton University Press, 1994, 85–265

Stepelevich, Lawrence S. "Max Stirner and Ludwig Feuerbach." *Journal of the History of Ideas*, Volume 39 (1978), pp. 451–463

-------- "Max Stirner as Hegelian." *Journal of the History of Ideas*, Volume 46 (1985), pp. 597–614

-------- "The Revival of Max Stirner." *Journal of the History of Ideas*, Volume 35, No. 2 (April-June, 1974), pp. 323–328

-------- (ed.) *The Young Hegelians: An Anthology*. Cambridge: Cambridge University Press, 1983

Strawson, PF. *Individuals*. London: Routledge, 1959

Tomba, Massimiliano. *Marx's Temporalities*. Leiden: Brill, 2013

Tucker, Benjamin R. *Instead of a Book, By a Man Too Busy To Write One*. Elibron Classics (facsimile of 1897 edition), 2005

Welsh, John F. *Max Stirner's Dialectical Egoism*. Lanham: Lexington Books, 2010

Wittgenstein, Ludwig. "Lecture on Ethics." *The Philosophical Review*, Volume 74, No. 1 (January 1965), pp. 3–12

Wood, Allen. *Hegel's Ethical Thought*. Cambridge: Cambridge University Press, 1990

Zero Books

CULTURE, SOCIETY & POLITICS

Contemporary culture has eliminated the concept and public figure of the intellectual. A cretinous anti-intellectualism presides, cheer-led by hacks in the pay of multinational corporations who reassure their bored readers that there is no need to rouse themselves from their stupor. Zer0 Books knows that another kind of discourse – intellectual without being academic, popular without being populist – is not only possible: it is already flourishing. Zer0 is convinced that in the unthinking, blandly consensual culture in which we live, critical and engaged theoretical reflection is more important than ever before.

If you have enjoyed this book, why not tell other readers by posting a review on your preferred book site.

Recent bestsellers from Zero Books are:

In the Dust of This Planet
Horror of Philosophy vol. 1
Eugene Thacker
In the first of a series of three books on the Horror of
Philosophy, *In the Dust of This Planet* offers the genre of horror
as a way of thinking about the unthinkable.
Paperback: 978-1-84694-676-9 ebook: 978-1-78099-010-1

Capitalist Realism
Is there no alternative?
Mark Fisher
An analysis of the ways in which capitalism has presented itself
as the only realistic political-economic system.
Paperback: 978-1-84694-317-1 ebook: 978-1-78099-734-6

Rebel Rebel
Chris O'Leary
David Bowie: every single song. Everything you want to know,
everything you didn't know.
Paperback: 978-1-78099-244-0 ebook: 978-1-78099-713-1

Cartographies of the Absolute
Alberto Toscano, Jeff Kinkle
An aesthetics of the economy for the twenty-first century.
Paperback: 978-1-78099-275-4 ebook: 978-1-78279-973-3

Malign Velocities
Accelerationism and Capitalism
Benjamin Noys
Longlisted for the Bread and Roses Prize 2015, *Malign Velocities* argues against the need for speed, tracking acceleration as the symptom of the ongoing crises of capitalism.
Paperback: 978-1-78279-300-7 ebook: 978-1-78279-299-4

Meat Market
Female Flesh under Capitalism
Laurie Penny
A feminist dissection of women's bodies as the fleshy fulcrum of capitalist cannibalism, whereby women are both consumers and consumed.
Paperback: 978-1-84694-521-2 ebook: 978-1-84694-782-7

Poor but Sexy
Culture Clashes in Europe East and West
Agata Pyzik
How the East stayed East and the West stayed West.
Paperback: 978-1-78099-394-2 ebook: 978-1-78099-395-9

Romeo and Juliet in Palestine
Teaching Under Occupation
Tom Sperlinger
Life in the West Bank, the nature of pedagogy and the role of a university under occupation.
Paperback: 978-1-78279-637-4 ebook: 978-1-78279-636-7

Sweetening the Pill
or How We Got Hooked on Hormonal Birth Control
Holly Grigg-Spall
Has contraception liberated or oppressed women? *Sweetening the Pill* breaks the silence on the dark side of hormonal contraception.
Paperback: 978-1-78099-607-3 ebook: 978-1-78099-608-0

Why Are We The Good Guys?
Reclaiming Your Mind from the Delusions of Propaganda
David Cromwell
A provocative challenge to the standard ideology that Western power is a benevolent force in the world.
Paperback: 978-1-78099-365-2 ebook: 978-1-78099-366-9